PIVOT POINT

PIVOT POINT FUNDAMENTALS: COSMETOLOGY
PERM & RELAX

1st Edition
4th Printing, October 2021
Printed in China

Pivot Point International, Inc.
Global Headquarters
8725 West Higgins Road, Suite 700
Chicago, IL 60631 USA

847-866-0500
pivot-point.com

CONTENTS

120

154

129

167

75

206

2

111^c.1// PERM THEORY

EXPLORE //

Think of someone you've known that has worn a perm at some time. How does that perm compare with the permed textures available in today's market?

INSPIRE //

Perm services change clients' everyday appearance, boost their confidence and can also be a significant revenue generator in the salon.

ACHIEVE //

Following this lesson on *Perm Theory,* you'll be able to:

>> State the breakthroughs that influenced the perm texture systems used today

>> Explain the two phases involved when performing a perm texture service

FOCUS //

PERM THEORY
History of Perming
Phases of Perming

111ᶜ.1 | PERM THEORY

Perming is a chemical texture service that involves the process of using physical and chemical actions to permanently change the texture of hair, giving your clients the straight-to-wavy or curly looks they desire.

Perms today are very different from the crunchy, frizzy and tightly curled perms you might have seen in past decades. There are texture and waving systems that create a variety of looks, from sexy, tousled waves to beautiful, soft and resilient curls. The science and technology of today's perms offer clients more than ever before, including the length of time the new texture lasts and options to wear both perm and hair color.

Clients often request a perm texture service:

» To add volume, texture and style support to flat, limp hair

» To add textural interest in selected areas or throughout the head

» To have the option of wearing their hair straight or textured

Perming is a service to be offered in conjunction with other salon services. Since the sculpted form is the foundation of every design composition, your clients will rely on you to perfectly integrate the haircut and the permed texture to achieve the desired look. When your client wants a look that requires added texture, consider how all the design elements of form, texture and color will work together.

HISTORY OF PERMING

The desire for curly or wavy hair dates back to ancient cultures. The ancient Egyptians wrapped hair around wooden sticks, applied mud from hot springs and then baked it in the sun. When the mud was dry, it was removed. Sometimes the results lasted a few weeks, possibly because of sulfur derivatives in the mud.

The ability to create long-lasting curls and waves, which today is called perming or permanent waving, became a reality in the 20th century.

In 1905, Charles Nessler made the first real breakthrough with his heat permanent waving machine:

>> Suitable for longer hair

>> Hair was wrapped tightly around heated rollers in a spiral fashion

>> **This spiral method involved wrapping the hair from scalp to ends**

The first permanents consisted of a solution of strong alkalis heated to about 212°F (100°C) with the aid of electrical heaters.

In 1926, **the croquignole method of wrapping hair from the ends to the scalp** was created to accommodate women who had cut their hair shorter after World War I.

The croquignole method:

>> **Also known as the overlap method**

>> **Led the way to the use of clamps that were preheated on a separate electric unit and then placed over the hair**

>> **This preheated clamp process was called the preheat or machineless method**

>> Strong alkaline chemicals were also used with heat to produce lasting curls

1930s

In 1931 at the Midwest Beauty Show in Chicago, Ralph I. Evans and Everett G. McDonough introduced a heatless technique of perming:

>> Used bisulfides instead of electricity

>> Process produced a chemical reaction that re-formed the hair from straight to curly or wavy

>> Sometimes the client would have the wave wrapped in the salon, go home and then return in the morning for her finished design, which led to the name the "overnight wave"

By 1938, Arnold F. Willatt had invented the first cold wave:

>> It was called "cold" because no machines were used

>> Chemicals created no heat reactions

>> **Hair was still wrapped on perm rods, while a waving lotion (thioglycolic acid or a derivative) processed the hair without heat**

>> After rinsing, a chemical with an acidic pH (neutralizer) was applied to re-form hair to take on the shape of the rod

1970s

Acid (buffered) waves appeared on the market in the early 1970s:

>> **Contained a thioglycolic derivative called glyceryl monothioglycolate**

>> Did not contain ammonia

>> **Heat added by placing a plastic cap on client's head and placing under a heated dryer**

>> **Called endothermic because heat is absorbed from the surroundings**

Today's acid perms are in a pH range of 6.9-7.2.

Exothermic perms generate their own heat through a chemical reaction:

>> Additive mixed with perm solution to cause reaction

>> Self-timing

>> Self-heating

>> Range from acid to alkaline

Perm products currently in the market include:

>> Neutral

>> Low pH alkaline

>> Low/no thio perms, which may or may not require heat

The 21st century brought about a new, innovative method of producing soft, wavy, loose-curled texture:

>> Sometimes referred to as a "Digital Perm," "hot perm" or "soft wave"

>> Originated in Japan

>> Uses heated rods and temperature-regulating machine to digitally control heat and set curl

>> Solution is applied only where wave is desired

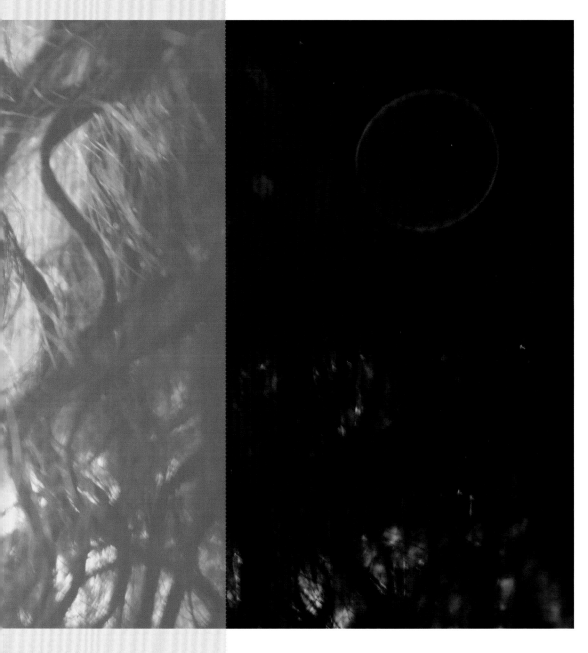

SALON**CONNECTION**

Modern Perms

Some of your clients may have outdated notions or ideas about perm services based on their past experiences or observations. With your knowledge of the possibilities of perms in today's salon, you can help these clients see new potential and how they might benefit from a perm service.

DISCOVER**MORE**

Perm trends have evolved over the years, from the short permed looks in the early part of the 20th century, to the perm boom of the 1980s to the soft, wavy and loosely curled looks we're seeing today. Research different perm trends throughout history and see if you can determine what factors might have influenced these trends.

PHASES OF PERMING

Today's perms generally involve two major phases:

- » Physical phase

- » Chemical phase

Physical Phase

Chemical Phase

Final Result

Both phases of the perm process are of equal importance.

PHYSICAL PHASE

In the physical phase of perming, the desired size and shape of the new wave or curl pattern are achieved by wrapping the hair around perm rods with corresponding sizes and shapes.

The hair needs to be wrapped:

- » Smoothly and evenly around each rod

- » Using appropriate tension without stretching hair to ensure the hair takes on the desired shape

Because wrapping the hair is key to achieving the final result and requires a significant amount of time, your skill in performing the physical phase is an important part of a successful perm service.

To perform the physical phase of a perm service, you'll need to be familiar with:

- » Distribute and section

- » Wrap
  - ▪ Perm rods (tools)
  - ▪ End-paper techniques
  - ▪ Base control
  - ▪ Perm patterns

CHEMICAL PHASE

The chemical phase begins after the hair has been wrapped on perm tools or rods. The chemical process transforms the hair into the lasting wavy or curly permed texture.

There are two chemicals used during the chemical phase:

>> Perm solution (reducing agent)

>> Neutralizer (oxidizing agent)

Perm solution:
>> Also known as waving lotion or reforming lotion

>> Applied to break disulfide bonds and soften protein structure:
  ▪ Allows the protein chains to assume shape of perm rod

Neutralizer:
>> Applied after perm solution is thoroughly rinsed

>> Applied to reharden and fix hair into new wavy or curly shape, then thoroughly rinsed

You'll learn more about perm solutions and neutralizers in the upcoming lesson, *Perm Products and Essentials.*

Specialized perm skills will allow you to transform and personalize a client's appearance by supporting or enhancing their hair sculpture.

LESSONS LEARNED

>> Perming is a chemical texture service offered in the salon that transforms hair from straight to wavy or curly.

- In 1905, Charles Nessler made the first real breakthrough with his heat permanent waving machine.

- In 1938, Arnold F. Willatt had invented the first cold wave–a machineless method which used a waving lotion, thioglycolic acid or a derivative.

- Acid waves appeared on the market in the early 1970s, which contained thioglycolic derivative called glyceryl monothioglycolate.

>> There are two phases involved when performing a perm:

- Physical phase – The desired size and shape of the new wave or curl pattern are achieved by wrapping the hair around perm rods with corresponding sizes and shapes.

- Chemical phase – Perm solution is applied to hair to break the hair's internal bonds. Neutralizer is applied to reharden and fix the hair into a lasting wavy or curly permed texture.

111ᶜ.2 //
PERM DESIGN

Do you think it's important to customize perm designs when adding texture to a client's hair?

INSPIRE //

When you use different effects and patterns to personalize your client's texture, you'll grow as a professional.

ACHIEVE //

Following this lesson on *Perm Design*, you'll be able to:

>> Summarize a series of design decisions involved when adding texture that will lead to a desired texture result

>> Identify the most commonly used basic perm patterns

FOCUS //

PERM DESIGN

Perm Design Decisions

Perm Patterns

Change the Texture, Change the Effect

111ᶜ.2 |
PERM DESIGN

To get from a perm design you have in mind to a final result that matches your mental picture takes a series of decisions. Each of those decisions will have an effect on the final perm design result. Adding texture influences the shape of the existing form.

PERM DESIGN DECISIONS

Before reaching for a perm product or perm tools, the designer must first visualize the final texture outcome. With that picture in mind, the designer then makes specific decisions based on the following questions:

>> What is the existing and desired texture?

>> What form will I be working with?

>> Where will I position the texture?

>> Which design principle will I use?

EXISTING AND DESIRED TEXTURE

As the name implies, the texture change created by perming is permanent; it is difficult to reverse or change afterward. Therefore, always thoroughly consult with clients about the size and character of their new curls or waves and show visual examples.

Size or Character

In perming, the basic decision when moving from the client's existing texture to the desired texture includes the following:

» Type of texture desired determines size and character (shape) of perm rods:
  - Tight, firm curls
  - Large, loose curls
  - Waves, or spiral curls

» Technique used to wrap the hair around the rods

There are two basic wrapping techniques for rotating strands of hair around a perm tool: overlap and spiral.

Overlap (croquignole) technique:

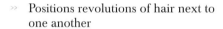

» Produces curls and undulating waves

» Achieves base lift, strong end curl

» Best suited for short- to medium-length hair

Spiral technique:

» Positions revolutions of hair next to one another

» Creates an elongated texture pattern

» Consistent along the length of the strand

» Most often used on medium to long hair

FORM

As you progress through the decision-making process for adding texture, use your imagination to visualize the possible outcomes of each decision along the way.

Consider:

» The relationship between form and texture

» How desired form and texture interplay with one another to create total composition

» Amount of additional length reduction that will occur when the hair is permed

As added texture expands the form:

» Illusion of shorter length is created

» Form line and weight area shift upward

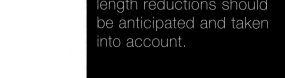

When adding texture, the hair is often sculpted before beginning the chemical process, so length reductions should be anticipated and taken into account.

The following examples show how the addition of wavy and curly textures affects the same length arrangement.

SOLID FORM

INCREASE-LAYERED FORM

COMBINATION FORM

TEXTURE PLACEMENT

One of the biggest misconceptions about perm designing is the idea that the client's hair must all be permed the same way. Placing texture in one or more specific areas or zones of the head, or along only a certain portion of the hairstrand, can produce a variety of interesting and innovative results.

Texture Within Zones

Zonal or partial perms position added texture within specific areas of a design to:

>> Emphasize specific areas of a hair sculpture

>> Add subtle support to specific areas

>> Create a bold statement

Look at the following examples.

Adding texture to the fringe can add volume and height to otherwise straight hair.

Texture added along the perimeter is ideal for face-framing textures.

Add texture to the interior to elongate the form and create height.

SALON**CONNECTION**

Customize

By customizing a perm design, you can create the texture that your client wants, accentuate their hair sculpture and make it easier for your client to style at home. That's a win-win!

DISCOVER**MORE**

From runways to editorial fashion shoots, there's a "texture revolution" going on and product companies, as well as industry leaders, are staking their claim.

Skilled texture specialists are being sought out for great career opportunities. Research to find which industry front-runners are offering texture education classes, with emphasis on designing with texture.

Texture Along the Strand

Texture may be added along the entire strand from base to ends, as in classic perming designs, or along specific portions of the strand to achieve a variety of customized effects.

BASE

Adding texture only at the base, called **base perming**, is usually done for one of two reasons:

1. To create lift and volume for added fullness and support of the overall hair design

2. More commonly, to add texture to new hair growth in order to match previously permed texture along the strand

AWAY FROM THE BASE

Adding texture away from the base, or end perming, creates contrasting textures that can result in progressive designs or a natural-looking finish. The proportional amount of texture added is determined according to the final desired effect.

DIRECTION

Another aspect of your perm design decisions will relate to the direction in which your client will wear his or her hair. There are four main ways to distribute hair for a perm:

Away From the Face　　*Toward the Face*　　*From a Side Part*　　*Alternating Clockwise and Counterclockwise Directions*

DESIGN PRINCIPLES AND ROD CHOICE

As a hair designer, you'll use the design principles when envisioning perm designs for clients. You can apply the following design principles to texture within zones, along a strand or throughout an entire composition. You can use each design principle on its own or in combination with others to create unique, customized designs.

Repetition

Repeating the same shape and diameter perm rod throughout the perm design creates a repetitive texture, which is often desired in classic designs. Repetition works well for designs that will be maintained with a roller set.

Alternation

Alternating rod diameters or rod shapes creates a mix of textures, and depending on the degree of difference between the tools, results can range from natural-looking finishes to dramatic effects.

Progression

A progression of rod diameters can create a large-to-small or small-to-large texture pattern. This is often chosen to create design emphasis or to adjust to different lengths within the hair sculpture.

Contrast

Extreme differences can be created by positioning the texture only in a selected area of a design or along a portion of the hairstrand.

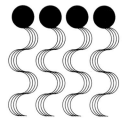

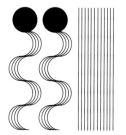

PERM PATTERNS

"Perm pattern" is the term used to refer to the way perm tools are arranged around the client's head while wrapping.

Perm patterns:
>> Also known as wrapping patterns

>> Help you organize and control how your perm service is performed

>> Affect the final look of the new curl pattern

Any perm pattern can, and often must, be adapted to suit the size and shape of an individual client's head. The basic shapes, as well as the shapes of the bases within those shapes, may need to be altered. This allows the rods to fit better without pulling away from the head or causing excessive shifting. If the rods are not positioned properly in relation to their bases, the result can be weaker bases with uneven support.

Of the many possible perm patterns, the most commonly used are:

- Rectangle pattern
- Contour pattern
- One-two bricklay pattern
- Spiral bricklay pattern
- Zonal pattern

RECTANGLE PATTERN
>> Also known as 9-block

>> Consists primarily of rectangular sections subdivided into rectangular bases

>> Center rectangle usually positioned front hairline to nape

>> Usually wrapped in downward direction

>> Front of center rectangle can be wrapped away from or toward face

>> Sides generally subdivided in half with rectangle bases throughout

>> Rod position may vary, but wrapping downward from horizontal bases facilitates quick wrapping

>> Generally considered the most basic perm pattern and can be performed on any sculpted form

>> Adjustment can be made in rod type, diameter, position and application for varied results

>> Larger diameter rods are often chosen when wrapping rectangle pattern on longer lengths

CONTOUR PATTERN

>> Versatile and adapts to contours or curves of head

>> Includes a central rectangle and two sections at each side

>> Indirect partings from multiple points of origin are used in sections adjacent to center rectangle

>> Diagonal-forward partings gradually become horizontal toward back and exterior, following contours of head; sometimes diagonal-back at nape

>> Remaining side section most commonly wrapped using diagonal-forward or diagonal-back partings; other directions may be used

BRICKLAY PATTERN

>> Positions rods in a staggered configuration to avoid splits

>> Bases within each row are offset from previous row so vertical lines do not line up

>> Pattern resembles the way a bricklayer deliberately arranges the bricks in a building, alternating their position row by row

>> Generally uses rectangle-shaped and trapezoid-shaped bases, which can be positioned in any direction, usually horizontally and diagonally, depending upon curves of head

>> Wrapped with overlap technique

>> Used to create consistent curl

>> Helps avoid splits between bases

One-Two Method

>> Wrapping begins at center of each row with one or two rods

>> Entire row completed before moving to next row

>> Bases naturally stagger to create bricklay pattern

Any application that staggers bases will avoid splits, but the one-two method is most commonly used.

SPIRAL BRICKLAY PATTERN

>> Features horizontal rows that are subdivided in a staggered bricklay pattern

>> Rods are positioned vertically within rectangular bases

>> Used in conjunction with one-two bricklay pattern

>> Usually wrapped ends-to-base; can be base-to-ends if rod requires

>> Common to alternate wrapping directions and rod diameters

>> Shorter exterior lengths can be wrapped with overlap technique

>> Achieves an elongated curl pattern on medium to longer lengths of hair

ZONAL PATTERN

>> Zonal perms; also called partial perms

>> Involves adding texture in certain areas or zones of head

>> Adds volume and directional movement to otherwise straight hair in selected areas

>> Works well for clients with short hair

>> Generally used in areas such as fringe, crown and nape

>> Added texture may harmonize or contrast existing texture

CHANGE THE TEXTURE, CHANGE THE EFFECT

With your training as a hair designer, you'll have the power to transform your clients' appearance. Most clients, particularly those with straight hair, will ask you for more volume when seeking changes for their hair. Notice the changes created by expanding the volume in the examples shown here and the effect on each client's image.

LESSONS LEARNED

Adding texture expands the form and can create the illusion of shorter length.

When adding texture, the hair is often sculpted before beginning the chemical process.

Partial or zonal perms incorporate texture within a specific zone or area of the head for various effects from adding subtle support to creating bold statements.

Texture may be added along the entire strand from base to ends or along specific portions of the strand to achieve a variety of customized effects.

You can apply design principles to texture within zones, along a strand or throughout an entire composition.

"Perm pattern" is the term used to refer to the way perm rods are arranged around the client's head while wrapping.

The most commonly used perm patterns are:
>> Rectangle pattern

>> Contour pattern

>> One-two bricklay pattern

>> Spiral bricklay pattern

>> Zonal pattern

As you progress through the decision-making process for transforming texture, use your imagination to visualize the possible outcomes of each decision along the way.

Carefully considered design decisions will allow you to envision beautiful perm designs for your clients and to achieve the most effective results.

111ᶜ.3 //

PERM PRODUCTS AND ESSENTIALS

EXPLORE //

From springy, bouncy curls to sexy, loose waves—what types of perms and perm tools do you think you will use to achieve the looks you and your clients envision?

INSPIRE //

There is no "one-perm-fits-all" perm product on the market, so choosing the right type of perm and the most appropriate perm tools takes some effort.

ACHIEVE //

Following this lesson on *Perm Products and Essentials,* you'll be able to:

>> Explain the types of perm products and their usage

>> Describe the functions of the main tools used for perming

>> Provide examples of products, tools and equipment used to perform a perm service

FOCUS //

PERM PRODUCTS AND ESSENTIALS

Perm Products

Perm Essentials

111°.3 | PERM PRODUCTS AND ESSENTIALS

Each client who requests a perm has a unique head of hair with various hair and scalp conditions. Determining the most appropriate perm solution for a client—whether color-treated with coarse texture, or fine texture with resistant porosity—will be simpler with knowledge of the types of perm solutions.

PERM PRODUCTS

Perms (or permanent waving) allow you to chemically reform hair from straight to a wavy or curly formation.

>> Hair is wrapped around perm rods chosen to reflect desired curl pattern

>> Processing (waving) lotion is applied to break disulfide bonds

  ▪ Softens protein structure

  ▪ Allows protein chains to assume shape of perm tool

>> Rinsing removes processing lotion

>> Second chemical product, neutralizer (rebonding lotion), reforms disulfide bonds in new configuration

The resulting chemical change in the hair holds the hair in the new position or curl pattern.

Original Straight Hair

Shifting and Breaking of Disulfide Bonds

Disulfide Bonds Reformed

TYPES OF PERM SOLUTIONS (LOTIONS)

Manufacturers have made a wide variety of perm solutions available. This enables you to select the most appropriate solution–based on your pre-perm analysis of your client's hair and the strength of the curl desired.

There are two general categories of perms used in the salon:

» Alkaline (Cold) Perms – Processed without heat

» Acid (Heat) Perms – Generally processed with heat

ALKALINE (COLD) PERMS	ACID (HEAT) PERMS
Perm solution chemically breaks or reduces the strong disulfide bonds while hair is wrapped on perm rods.	Heat, tension and perm solution break disulfide bonds.

BOTH ALKALINE AND ACID
Processing action softens protein structure and allows disulfide bonds to shift and assume shape of perm rod.

Alkaline Perms

Alkaline perms, also known as "cold waves," are processed without heat. They are an excellent choice for resistant hair or when strong curl patterns are desired. Before using an alkaline perm, it is important to know the following:

» **Alkaline perms have a pH of approximately 8.0-9.5.** The alkalinity softens and swells the hair fibers, making it easier for the chemicals to penetrate the hair structure.

» **The main ingredient found in alkaline waves is thioglycolic acid or its derivatives and ammonium hydroxide. Ammonium hydroxide is added to the formula to shorten the processing time.**

» **Because of the high alkalinity, it is necessary to use caution and skill to prevent damage to the hair structure or chemical burns to the skin.**

» Alkaline perms are not recommended for highly porous hair.

» **Alkaline perms should be wrapped without tension (minimal stretching or straining of the hair)** because alkaline reforming lotion causes the hair to swell, creating the necessary tension on the hair.

» Hair should be held taut enough to control the hair, creating a smooth, even wrap from ends to scalp.

» Wrapping the hair with too much tension could result in an uneven penetration of the lotion and lead to breakage.

» Because the hair swells, it is easier to rinse and blot the hair when using an alkaline perm.

» **The hair starts to process as soon as the solution is applied.**

Remember – Alkaline perms are applied without heat.

The low-pH alkaline perm is created for textures and types of hair that do not respond well to other kinds of perm solutions. With a pH of 8, it's less alkaline than the typical cold perm.

Acid Perms

Acid perms, also known as "heat perms," are processed with heat.
Acid perms are slower acting than alkaline perms and recommended for damaged, highly porous and previously permed hair. Before using an acid perm, it is important to know the following:

» **Acid perms are in the pH range of 6.9-7.2.**

» Acid perms in the market today are now capable of processing without heat. They start with a higher pH, and heat is an option for a firmer curl.

» **Acid perms cause only minimal swelling, therefore it is essential that the hair be wrapped with firm, even tension.**

» Heat and wrapping with even tension boost the penetration of the glyceryl monothioglycolate into the hairstrands, where it breaks the disulfide bonds.

» Without uniform tension throughout the strand, the perm will not process correctly, which may produce an uneven curl pattern.

» The heat needed for acid perms is often just the client's body heat that is trapped by placing a plastic bag over the perm wrap. Additional heat is achieved by placing the client under a hood dryer.

» Since the lower pH of an acid perm requires longer processing time, there is less chance of damage from overprocessing; however, you still want to monitor the process carefully.

» It is essential to completely rinse the perm solution from the hair before neutralizing. Since acid perms cause little swelling, it takes more time (at least five minutes) and attention to remove the perm solution from the hair than with an alkaline perm.

» Insufficient rinsing before neutralizing can trap odor in the hair.

Advantages of Alkaline and Acid Perms

ALKALINE PERMS	ACID PERMS
Strong curl pattern	Soft, natural curl pattern
Faster processing time	Gentler to hair
Better for resistant hair	More control due to slower processing time
No need for heat	Better for fragile or chemically treated hair

EXOTHERMIC PERMS

Exothermic perms are self-heating and self-timing. An additive is mixed with the perm solution to create heat through a chemical reaction. The pH can vary, so they can be either alkaline or acid, depending on the manufacturer. Exothermic perms are available for all types of hair and have similar benefits to acid perms.

LOW/NO THIO

The low/no thio perm, introduced in 1992, has a different reducing agent known as cystemine hydrochloride (hi-dro-**CLOR**-ide). It is available to people who may have an allergic reaction to thioglycolic acid, which is found in both alkaline and acid perms.

There are many benefits to using this type of perm:

>> Deeper penetration of the solution for longer-lasting and more consistent curls

>> Less dilation of the cuticle layer

>> The ability to reform up to 60% more bonds during neutralization

IONIC/HEAT PERMS

A recent type of perm available is often referred to as a "heat" perm. These perms make use of a computer to digitally control the temperature of each perm rod, giving the stylist a greater degree of control over the whole perming process. This type of perm is popular in many Asian and European countries and is gaining popularity in the U.S.

The heat perm:

>> Is also referred to as a "hot perm," "ionic perm," "soft wave" or "digital perm"

>> Generally produces soft-looking waves and curls, which are more defined when dry and looser when wet

>> Thermally reconditions the hair using the perm solution and heated rods

>> Generally does not require curling creams, pomades or gels to achieve curl

>> Lasts 3-6 months depending on hair

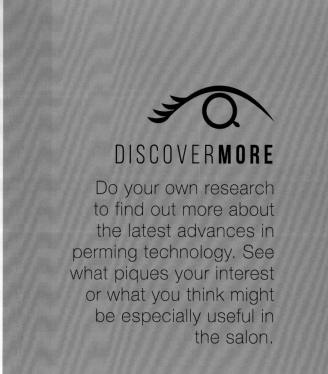

DISCOVER**MORE**

Do your own research to find out more about the latest advances in perming technology. See what piques your interest or what you think might be especially useful in the salon.

NEUTRALIZER

Neutralizing is the final chemical step in the perm process. The following is important to know about neutralizer:

>> It reforms the disulfide bonds while lowering the pH of the hair

>> **The main ingredient found in most neutralizers (or bonding lotions) is either hydrogen peroxide, sodium perborate or sodium bromate**

   ▪ If left on longer than specified by the manufacturer, all three can cause damage to the hair, such as drying it out or, in severe cases, causing breakage

>> **The pH can range from 2.5 to 7, depending on the type of neutralizer**

>> Neutralizing is also known as rebonding or oxidation

>> **Reduces the swelling caused by the alkalinity of the perm solution and rebonds and restores the disulfide bonds**

>> **Rehardens, or fixes, the disulfide bonds into the new shifted position, which is determined by the size of the perm rod, making the texture change "permanent"**

BARRIER/PROTECTIVE CREAMS

Before applying the perm solution, a barrier cream is applied to protect the skin.

Barrier cream:

>> Also known as base cream

>> Petroleum is main ingredient

>> Applied to the hairline and ears

>> Helps hold cotton in place

>> Helps protect skin from perm solution

Protective cream is applied to areas of the hair that are not being processed. Protective cream prevents the perm solution from being absorbed into the hair.

The following summarizes the perm products and their related functions:

PRODUCTS	FUNCTION
Shampoo	Cleanses, removes dirt and oils from scalp and hair
Perm Solution	Reduces disulfide bonds so hair can assume new shape of perm rod
Neutralizer	Fixes, locks in, restores bonds to make new shape of hair permanent
Barrier Cream	Protects client's skin when applied to hairline before using chemicals
Protective Cream	Protects parts of hairstrand not being processed during a retouch service

It is interesting to know that oxygen from the air (air oxidation) can achieve the same results as the neutralizer. Air oxidation is impractical, however, because the hair must dry naturally on the perm rods, without heat, for 24-48 hours, depending on the length and texture of the hair.

Keep in mind, employers are required to make Safety Data Sheets (SDS) for all products available for your reference and use in the salon.

PERM ESSENTIALS

To deliver a professional perm service, you need an organized selection of tools. Perm service equipment includes furnishings and provisions necessary to provide a professional service.

PERM TOOLS

TOOLS	FUNCTION
Applicator Bottle	» Controls and applies perm solution or neutralizer » Nozzle or tip is used for better control of product being applied
Perm Rods	» Determine the size and shape of new curl configuration » Come in different diameters and shapes » Different diameters produce different degrees of curl activation
Styling Comb	» Controls, distributes and parts hair to be wrapped within a section
Tail Comb	» Parts off sections of hair and individual bases when wrapping

Both plastic and metal tail combs can be used when wrapping with water. However, metal tail combs *cannot* be used when pre-softening or wrapping with perm solution, as this could result in a negative chemical reaction.

NOTE:
Prior to examinations, check if a choice of a plastic or metal tail comb is allowed by your area's regulating agency.

PERM SUPPLIES

SUPPLIES	FUNCTION
Plastic Shampoo Cape	» Protects client from chemicals and water
Cloth Towels	» Absorb and remove water, perm solution and neutralizer through blotting
Perm Bib/Neutralizing Cape	» Catches excess chemicals as they run off the scalp; protects client
Cotton Strips	» Protect client's skin from chemicals when applied around hairline
Plastic Sectioning Clips	» Hold hair in place in controlled sections before and during wrapping procedure

SUPPLIES	FUNCTION
End Papers	>> Control the hair ends when wrapping >> Equalize porosity and absorbency during processing, rinsing and neutralizing
Picks/Stabilizers	>> Hold perm rods in position when placed under perm rod band >> Provide extra security during or after wrapping so that rods will not move during chemical phase >> Avoid band pressure on hair
Spray Bottle	>> Holds water used to keep hair damp for more control of hair while wrapping
Protective Gloves	>> Shield designer's hands from chemicals during processing

PERM EQUIPMENT

EQUIPMENT	FUNCTION
Heat Equipment: Plastic Cap, Infrared Lamps, Hood Dryer	Provides heat for acid perms during processing as required by manufacturer's directions
Plastic Cap	Prevents perm solution from drying out during processing and traps client's body heat
Timer	Alerts designer to check for test curls, processing and neutralizing times as recommended by the manufacturer
Shampoo Bowl	Holds client's head and hair for shampooing prior to service and for rinsing perm solution and neutralizer from hair
Styling Chair	Provides comfortable seat for client; adjustable for best working height

SALON**CONNECTION**

Unique Clients

Remember that not all of your perm clients will request a perm to achieve a curly look. Many may simply need the support that permed texture offers to support a desired style.

Understanding the types of perms available and the related tool choices enables you to make more informed choices for your clients based on the desired end results.

LESSONS LEARNED

There are two general categories of perms used in the salon:

» Alkaline (cold) perms – Processed without heat
  - Also known as "cold waves"
  - Processed without heat
  - Good choice for resistant hair or when strong curl patterns are desired
  - pH of approximately 8.0-9.5

» Acid (heat) perms – Processed with heat
  - Also known as "heat perms"
  - Processed with heat
  - Slower acting than alkaline perms
  - Recommended for damaged, highly porous and previously permed hair
  - pH range of 6.9-7.2

Other products used in perm services are base cream and neutralizer.

The tools used to perform perm services include applicator bottles, perm rods, tail comb and styling comb.

Perm essentials include the supplies and equipment that are needed to perform a perm service.

» Supplies include cape, cloth towels, end papers, sectioning clips and protective gloves

» Equipment includes permanent fixtures such as the hydraulic chair, timer and shampoo bowl

111ᶜ.4 //
PERM SKILLS

EXPLORE //

Being skilled requires knowledge, training, and practice. Have you ever practiced something over and over until it became a skill?

INSPIRE //

Dedication and practice in all aspects of perming build your expertise and confidence, which will result in a loyal perm clientele.

ACHIEVE //

Following this lesson on *Perm Skills,* you'll be able to:

>> Explain how the hair is analyzed prior to a perm service

>> Identify and explain the procedural steps during the physical and chemical phases of a perm service

FOCUS //

PERM SKILLS

Pre-Perm Analysis

Perm Procedures

111°.4 | PERM SKILLS

Careful analysis of your client's hair, and your ability to apply the necessary perm skills, will allow you to create beautiful and successful perm designs for your clients. In *Perm Skills*, you'll focus on pre-perm analysis and the procedural steps used to carry out your design plans.

PRE-PERM ANALYSIS

It is important to perform a pre-perm analysis before any perm service. An analysis of the porosity, elasticity, texture and density of the client's hair will help you:

>> Choose the right base size and rod size for optimum curl development

>> Select the proper perm solution for effective results

>> Manage processing time safely and efficiently

POROSITY

Porosity refers to the ability of the hair to absorb moisture, liquids or chemicals. The more porous the hair is, the more able it is to absorb the perm solution.

Extreme Porosity

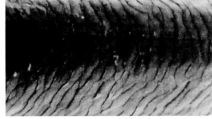

Resistant Porosity

The following are guidelines to use when perming hair with various types of porosity:

>> Porous hair:
  ▪ Mild acid perm is recommended

>> "Resistant" hair:
  ▪ Lacks porosity

  ▪ Requires stronger alkaline solution in order to pre-soften cuticle and allow perm chemicals to be absorbed

>> Highly or excessively porous hair:
  ▪ Usually in some stage of chemical or physical damage from highly alkaline shampoos, hair color treatments or thermal styling

  ▪ Needs to be reconditioned before any perm service with pre-wrapping product to equalize porosity

  ▪ Need to select gentler, slower-acting type of perm for greater control during processing

The following test, also known as a finger test, will help you determine hair porosity.

POROSITY TEST

>> Run your thumb and finger along a strand of hair against the direction of growth (ends to base). If the hair feels rough it will be due to the cuticle scales being raised and open, which is an indication that the hair is more porous and therefore damaged.

>> Record results in client's record.

ELASTICITY

Elasticity is the hair's ability to stretch and return to its original shape without breaking. Normal dry hair is capable of being stretched about ⅕ (20%) of its length. Wet hair is able to be stretched 40%-50% of its length. If hair has poor elasticity, it will not return to its original state after it is gently stretched.

Hair that lacks elasticity (also referred to as resiliency) can react adversely to perm solution, so it is not advisable or safe to perm hair that is weak or shows any signs of breakage.

Elasticity Test (Structural Strength)

While visual examination for elasticity is not absolutely accurate, it can tell you a great deal. By looking at and handling the hair, you'll make judgments about what it needs. The purpose of an **elasticity test, also known as the pull test**, is to check the ability of the hair to stretch and return to its original shape without breaking. The following test assesses any damage to the internal structure of the hair (cortex), prior to a chemical or styling service. Note that this test is intended for straight or wavy hair:

» Remove strand of hair from side of head, above ears

» Hold hair between thumb and forefinger; with thumbnail and index finger of other hand, run distance of hair rapidly (as when curling a ribbon with scissors); creates a series of small curls

» Gently pull hair taut for 10 seconds and release

If hair completely, or almost completely, returns to curl pattern, it's in good condition. If it returns only 50% or less, it's structurally weak and needs conditioning.

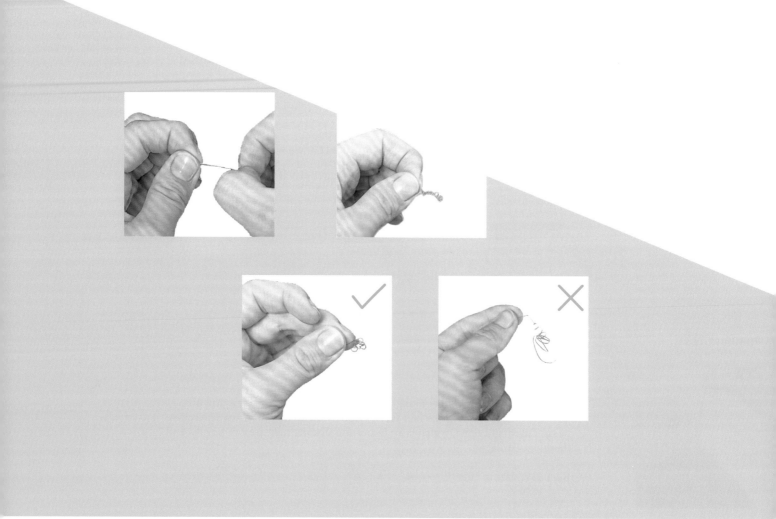

TEXTURE

You may remember from an earlier lesson that **the degree of coarseness or fineness in the hair fiber is referred to as texture**. The texture of hair is often categorized as either fine, medium or coarse. It is essential for you to consider texture in this way so you can select both the proper perm formula and size of perm tool or rod for your client's hair.

Although not always true, you will usually find that fine and coarse hair are more challenging to perm than hair with medium texture. Manufacturers will often label their perm products according to the results you can achieve for fine, medium or coarse hair.

| Fine hair may be resistant because of the tightly packed cuticle. | Medium hair has on average 7-12 layers of cuticle and generally accepts products well. | Coarse hair may be resistant due to the increased number of cuticle layers. |

Tenacity is a term meaning the ease or difficulty with which a product can penetrate the cuticle layer of the hair.

DENSITY

Density describes the amount of hair follicles per square inch on the scalp and is usually referred to as light, medium or heavy (thin, medium or thick). Hair density does not always correspond to hair texture. Hair with a fine texture can be very dense (thick) or not very dense (thin). Likewise, hair with a coarse texture is not necessarily dense, but can be thick or thin.

Analyzing the density of the hair helps determine the amount of hair that will be wrapped on each perm rod in the following ways:

>> Amount of hair placed on perm rod directly affects absorption of perm solution and neutralizer

>> Making adjustments for density of each client's hair is important for proper sectioning and wrapping

>> Denser hair will require smaller base sizes to ensure that there is not too much hair wrapped around the perm rods

Analyzing your client's hair and choosing the desired curl formation will help you select the appropriate perm products for your client and make appropriate decisions on how to section, wrap and process the hair to achieve the best results.

Manufacturers label their perm products according to hair texture, porosity and desired curl.

Texture:	Fine, medium, coarse
Porosity:	Normal, resistant, previously permed, tinted, bleached
Desired Curl:	Firm, true to tool size, soft body waves

PERM PROCEDURES

Before beginning any perm, you'll visualize an end result based on your client's needs and then make design decisions that lead to achieving the result. With a clear plan for the perm design, the next step is to carry out your plan using techniques that ensure predictable perm results. Combining these techniques with the design principles, you will be able to produce the perm designs you have envisioned for your clients.

The steps for performing a perm service are fairly consistent, no matter which perm pattern and wrapping techniques you are using. Note that the first three steps are part of the physical phase of perming, and the last two steps are part of the chemical phase.

PERM PROCEDURES
To perform consistent and reliable perm services, you can rely on this five-step procedure for predictable results:

PHYSICAL PHASE

Distribute   *Section*   *Wrap*

CHEMICAL PHASE

Process   *Neutralize*

DISTRIBUTE

Part of visualizing a finished perm result is seeing the direction in which the client will wear their hair. With this in mind, the first step in creating the perm is for you to direct, or distribute, the hair in that direction. This prepares the hair to be sectioned and then wrapped. There are four main ways to distribute hair:

AWAY FROM THE FACE

>> Hair is directed away from face

>> Ideal for clients who want to wear hair swept up or off face for a fresh look

TOWARD THE FACE

>> For clients wishing to wear a fringe

>> Direct hair toward face to frame eyes or create a focal point in finished design

FROM A SIDE PART

>> Ideal for clients who wish to wear hair from a chosen or natural side part

>> Direct hair downward from a side part to create an asymmetrical design; can drape over eye on heavier side

ALTERNATING CLOCKWISE AND COUNTERCLOCKWISE DIRECTIONS

>> Distribute hair in curved clockwise and counterclockwise directions to achieve alternating movements

>> Alternating directions are ideal for enhancing natural wave patterns or creating smooth, flowing waves

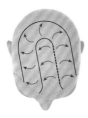  

SECTION

Prior to wrapping a perm, the head is often divided into several large sections for control. At first, you will section with a comb and use sectioning clips to secure the sections. With more experience, you will be able to visualize these divisions and section as you wrap.

Sections help you define and create bases, which are the areas between two partings. The shape of a base is largely determined by the shape of the section it is in. Perm rods are positioned according to these subsections or bases.

The main types, or shapes, of sections are:

RECTANGULAR

>> Rectangular sections

>> Rectangular bases

>> Often positioned through center front; may continue to center back

CIRCULAR

>> Circular sections

>> Triangular and trapezoidal bases

>> Can be used to accommodate curves of head

>> Can blend between other shapes

OBLONG

>> Oblong sections

>> Rhomboid-shaped bases

>> Can be positioned anywhere on head

>> Waves created when oblongs are positioned in alternating directions

WRAP

The most physical part of the perm service includes the actual application and positioning of the perm rods. It is essential to understand wrapping techniques and the effects of base control, which include:

>> Size of base in relation to rod diameter

>> Position of rod in relation to base

This will ensure that your final design result reflects the desired curl pattern, degree of base strength and directional emphasis that you and your client want.

Wrapping Techniques

There are two basic wrapping techniques for rotating strands of hair around a perm rod:

>> Overlap, also called croquignole

>> Spiral

OVERLAP TECHNIQUE

The overlap technique is the process of rotating or revolving hair around a tool from the ends of the hairstrand up to the base. With the overlap (croquignole) technique:

>> Hair overlaps itself with each revolution

>> Strand should overlap around perm rod at least 2.5 times to create complete curl pattern

>> Produces curls and undulating waves; also used to achieve base lift and strong end curl

>> Best suited for short- to medium-length hair

A version of the overlap technique is the **piggyback**, which positions two or more perm tools along the length of a single strand, either to create consistent texture on longer hair or to create more than one texture along the strand. With the piggyback technique:

>> First tool is wrapped like a base perm with the ends left loose

>> Second tool is wrapped in the opposite direction and positioned on top of the first tool

>> Reduces amount of hair around one rod allowing better saturation of chemicals

SPIRAL TECHNIQUE

The spiral wrapping technique is a method of wrapping the hair around a perm tool base-to-ends or ends-to-base; results in a corkscrew-shaped curl. With the spiral technique:

>> Revolutions of hair are positioned next to one another to create an elongated texture pattern

>> Texture pattern is consistent along length of strand and reflects shape and diameter of rods used

>> Best suited for medium to long hair

Hair can be wrapped in one of two ways:

>> Ends-to-base spiral – Place rod at end of hairstrand, then rotate under twice, move rod to a vertical position, wrap the hair around rod in corkscrew fashion to base, then secure

>> Base-to-ends spiral – Begin at base, wrap hair around rod, held vertically; secure when you reach end of strand

Perm Tools

TYPES OF RODS
Perm tools come in various lengths, diameters and shapes. The most common perm tool used is a perm rod. Perm rods are usually cylindrical in shape and generally straight or concave.

Straight perm rods produce curls or waves that are uniform throughout hairstrands.

- Hair on ends travels approximately same distance as hair in center, producing consistent curl pattern

Concave perm rods are a common perm tool that are narrower in the center and wider in diameter at the ends of the rod; produce a smaller tighter curl in the center.

- Hair on both ends travels farther to make one complete turn around rod than hair in center of rod

- Produce a wider, more spiraling pattern in hair wrapped around ends of rod

Large-diameter tools produce large curls, wave formations or body waves with a slow undulation.

» Work well when perming only certain areas of head (zonal or partial perm)

» Blend easily with unpermed areas

Medium-diameter tools produce texture with a faster rate or speed of activation than large-diameter tools.

» Results often described as curly or wavy

Small-diameter tools produce small, firm curls.

» Create fast texture with an energetic feeling

» Fast curl produced will greatly reduce appearance of hair's length

Soft rods are flexible tubes that allow hairstrands to be wrapped around the length of the tool to produce a natural-looking curl.

LENGTH REDUCTION

Analyzing the relationship between the hair length and the tool diameter will help you accurately anticipate the amount of length reduction that will take place. This chart represents the same length of hair permed on different diameter perm rods.

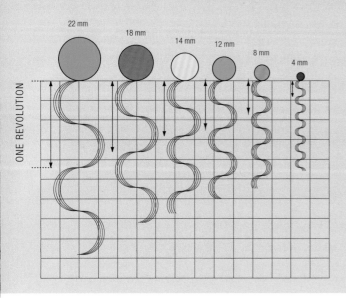

Notice that:

>> As permed texture is added by using smaller rods, hanging hair length becomes progressively shorter

>> Although hair itself does not actually become shorter, addition of permed texture creates *illusion* of shorter lengths

>> Number of revolutions hair makes around rod varies texture pattern
   - Large perm rod used on shorter hair achieves a loose wave; same rod used on longer hair produces a distinct undulation

Tool Position and Base Control

In perm, volume is the result of base lift, and base lift is the result of **base control**. Base control refers to the combination of two related aspects of perming:

1. The size of the base in relation to the diameter of the rod

2. The position of the rod in relation to the base

A base is the area between two partings for an individual perm tool. A base is also known as a panel, blocking or subsection.

BASE SIZE

Base size is defined by the base's length and width:
>> Length of base usually determined by length of perm rod being used.

>> If base is longer than length of rod, excess hair at both ends of rod will be dragged toward center; creates uneven curl pattern that is wider at both ends than it is in the center.

>> Width of base is determined by diameter of the perm rod being used.

>> A one diameter (1x) base size is equal to the tool's diameter.

>> When larger base sizes (such as 1½x and 2x) are used:
   ▪ More hair will be wrapped around rod
   ▪ Reduces amount of base lift
   ▪ Produces looser curl (which may be desired result)

>> Too much hair on perm rod:
   ▪ Will prevent solutions from penetrating properly, resulting in an uneven curl
   ▪ Can also cause tool bands to cut into or crease hair, which may produce a crimp or a ridge, causing a stress point on the hair, which in turn may eventually cause the hair to break

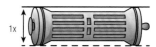

A 1x base size is most frequently used in perm design.

To achieve a 1½x base size, measure one full diameter plus one half.

A base that is measured with two full diameters of the chosen rod is called 2x base.

TOOL POSITION

Tool position refers to the placement of the wrapped perm rod in relation to its base.

It is determined by:
>> Size of base

>> Angle at which hair is projected while wrapping

Tool position affects the degree of lift from the base. Base lift creates volume, and many clients request a perm because they want more volume in their hair.

Tool position also affects the degree of blending between bases. There are four basic tool positions: on base, half-off base, underdirected and off base. They are described here in order from most base lift achieved to least base lift achieved.

ON BASE

On-base control is achieved with a 1x base size and the rod rests directly between the upper and lower partings. **On base is the tool position that creates the most volume** or base lift and is most often used in the interior or crown. This base control is not recommended for alkaline perms, since expansion is limited at the base and tension may cause breakage.

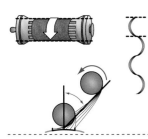  

From the 1x base, the hair is projected at 45° above the center of the base. This angle positions the rod directly on the base.

HALF-OFF BASE

The most commonly used base control is half-off base. **With half-off base control, the perm rod will be positioned half on its base and half-off its base, directly on the lower parting.** This base control creates medium base lift and allows for maximum blending between bases. Generally, a 1x base is used.

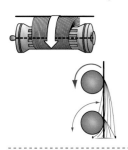  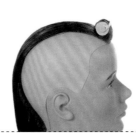

In this example, a 1x base is used. The hair is distributed and projected at 90° from the center of the base.

UNDERDIRECTED

Underdirected base control requires a base of at least 1½x and positions the rod in the lower half of the base. It results in moderate base lift and is often used in perimeter areas.

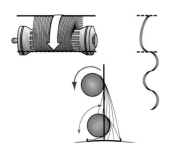  

In this example, a 1½x base is used. The hair is distributed and projected at 90° from the center of the base. Wrapping with this angle positions the rod in the lower part of the base for underdirected base control.

OFF BASE

Off-base control places the rod completely off of its base, resulting in minimal base lift. **An off-base tool placement is used only where you want a minimal degree of volume or base lift**, primarily near the perimeter for blending permed and unpermed areas.

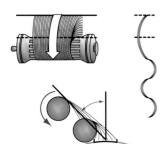 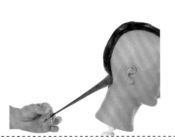 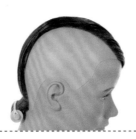

Although off-base control may be achieved with a larger base, a 1x base is used in this example. The hair is projected at 45° below the center of the base. This angle positions the rod completely off base.

End-Paper Techniques

End papers are used to control the hair ends and keep the hair smoothly wrapped around the perm rod, ensuring a smooth, uniform curl formation. End papers are available in several sizes and are chosen according to the hair length and the amount of hair being wrapped. These porous papers cover the ends of the hair to control uneven lengths, minimize breakage and eliminate crimps or "fishhooks" on the ends of the hair.

There are four basic techniques for applying end papers:

BOOKEND TECHNIQUE 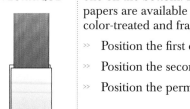	The **bookend technique** uses one end paper folded in half horizontally. This technique is generally used to control sections of hair when a shorter rod length is selected. The bookend technique is also used with larger end papers. » Position an end paper and fold it over the ends, or pre-fold an end paper and place it over the strand. » Slide the end paper partially past the ends of the strand without converging (bunching) the hair. Keep the ends of the hair flat and completely covered by the end paper. » **Optional:** Fold the end paper vertically, creating an elongated bookend technique, for longer hair or very narrow sections of hair. » Position the perm rod and wind.
DOUBLE-PAPER TECHNIQUE	The **double-paper (double-flat) technique** incorporates two end papers, one on the top of the strand and one on the bottom. It allows you maximum control of tapered ends and avoids bunching the ends. Longer end papers are available for this technique and are helpful for controlling large sections of hair and for protecting color-treated and fragile hair. » Position the first end paper under the strand, partially past the ends of the hair. » Position the second end paper on top of the strand, slightly past the first end paper. » Position the perm rod and wind.
SINGLE-PAPER TECHNIQUE	The **single-paper technique** is a more advanced version of the double-paper technique. It requires more practice because only one paper is used to control the ends of the hair. It is most often used on hair in good condition. » Position the end paper on top of the strand and slide it down partially past the ends. » Position the perm rod and wind.
CUSHION TECHNIQUE 	The **cushion technique** incorporates several end papers. It begins with a double-paper technique and then additional end papers are positioned on top of the strand as you wind the perm rod. This technique: » Layers end papers to provide cushioning and support to fragile hair » Controls shorter lengths within hair section » Is recommended for chemically treated or highly porous hair » Allows even absorption of processing solutions » Is used primarily in alkaline perming to keep hair smooth and provide for expansion when hair swells To perform this technique: » Position the first two end papers as in the double-paper technique. » Wind the perm rod to within ¼" (.6 cm) of the end of the first two papers. » Place another paper on top of the strand overlapping the first paper. » Wind the hair toward the base. Continue the cushion technique up the strand as needed.

When using multiple end papers, be sure to rinse and blot thoroughly since the extra papers hold more moisture than a single end paper. Water left in the end papers after rinsing the perm solution will dilute the neutralizer and weaken the curl formation.

Securing Perm Tools

The final part of the wrapping step is to ensure that all the perm rods are securely in their proper positions. Perm rods are secured:

>> Using stabilizers or picks

>> During or after wrapping the hair

>> So that the tools will not move or fall out of position during the chemical phase

Stabilizers or picks are usually placed in the same direction as the wrapping pattern. Securing also lifts the band off the hair to avoid band pressure.

Ergonomic Tips for Physical Phase of Perming

>> When wrapping the hair, stand directly behind the section to be wrapped, not to one side or the other.

>> Be sure the perm tools, end papers and spray bottle are within easy reach of your free hand. You will find it difficult to perform a smooth, even wrap if you need to shift to reach for supplies.

>> Do not bend over, stoop or raise your shoulders uncomfortably while wrapping. Raise or lower the styling chair and tilt the client's head to the proper angle. These adjustments help you keep your back erect, distribute weight evenly on your legs and eliminate shoulder cramps.

SALON**CONNECTION**

Getting Conditioned

Most clients who request a perm service are not aware that their hair should be in its very best condition before actually receiving the perm service. A little pre-perm care helps to ensure the best results. If necessary, regular conditioning treatments should be performed weeks before the perm service. Express to your clients that all conditioning treatments are not the same and that some are used to treat various hair conditions. Conditioning treatments need to be performed by a professional who will assess the condition of the hair to determine what the hair needs.

The last two perm procedures–process and neutralize–take place during the chemical phase of the service.

PROCESS

The chemical phase begins once the hair has been wrapped on perm tools.

Applying

After the hair has been wrapped, the processing solution should be applied carefully, one perm rod at a time. Ensure that the chemical solution thoroughly and evenly penetrates the hair on each rod for a consistent curl result. Missing rods will also produce an inconsistent curl formation. Follow manufacturer's instructions regarding processing. If the manufacturer's directions state that heat is required for processing, a plastic bag should be attached around the hairline and the client should be placed under a hood dryer. Heat is sometimes required for acid perms but generally not for alkaline perms. Resistant hair may require heat and a longer processing time.

Pay close attention to the amount of time the processing solution remains on the hair before rinsing. If left on too long, the result can be breakage, frizzy ends or weak curl formation.

An accurate perm pattern and smoothly wrapped hair will allow for proper saturation of the perm solution. Once the hair is wrapped:

» Barrier cream is applied around client's hairline.

» Cotton is positioned on top of barrier cream.

» Cotton should be replaced when it becomes saturated. Leaving the saturated cotton on the client's skin could cause chemical burns.

Timing and Testing

Getting the desired texture result depends on leaving the perm solution on the hair for the correct amount of time. Some perms are designed by the manufacturer to be self-timing. When using a self-timing perm, be sure to set a timer for the amount of time recommended by the manufacturer.

For perms that are not self-timing, you will need to test the hair to determine when processing is complete. A test curl allows you to see how well the bonds are softening and shifting to their new shape. To perform a test curl:

» Unwind 1½-2 turns of the rod, allowing hair to unfold naturally.

» Do not push hair toward head in an attempt to force desired curl formation to appear.

» If processing is complete, you should see a definite S-shape or pattern that tends to subdivide into groupings and the wave dimension should match the diameter of the perm rod. This is known as a positive test curl.

Rinsing

After processing is complete, as evidenced by a positive test curl, rinse the hair thoroughly with water per the manufacturer's instructions. To ensure client comfort and safety, follow best practices when rinsing perm tools by keeping one finger under the faucet to test and monitor the water temperature. Temporarily remove the glove on one hand to test the temperature of the water then place it back on prior to rinsing.

>> Rinsing stops processing action and removes all of perm solution from hair before neutralizing.

>> Some perms require a full five minutes for rinsing.

>> Long or thick hair may require more rinsing time.

>> Take care not to disturb the position of perm rods while rinsing because hair is in a swollen and softened state.

>> Use gentle water pressure to avoid disturbing hair on perm rods.

>> Be aware of water temperature; hot water will cause client discomfort, scalp irritation and can result in a tighter curl.

Blotting

After the perm lotion is thoroughly rinsed from the hair, you will blot the top and bottom of each perm rod with a towel to remove excess water. This is important because excess water left in the hair before neutralizing dilutes the neutralizer chemical and results in incomplete rebonding. Insufficient blotting, therefore, can lead to weak curls that relax sooner than they should.

NEUTRALIZE

Applying

Thoroughly saturate the hair on each perm tool with the neutralizing solution, applying to both sides of each rod. Follow manufacturer's instructions and be careful not to leave the neutralizer on the hair longer than recommended. This might dry out the hair or, in severe cases, cause breakage.

Rinsing

After the hair is neutralized, it needs to be rinsed with water again to remove all chemicals. Handle the hair carefully while rinsing because it is still swollen and can be easily damaged. There are two methods for rinsing the neutralizer:

1. Leave perm rods in position and thoroughly rinse neutralizer for a stronger curl result.

2. Remove perm rods, work neutralizer through to the ends, then rinse.

The chemical phase is now complete and the hair will retain the shape of the rods, resulting in a new texture configuration.

Understanding the procedures and practicing the skills involved in perm services will help you expand your expertise as well as your client base.

DISCOVER**MORE**

New perm technologies are changing perming procedures and expanding the possible results. Research the latest advances in the perm market and see how you may have to adapt the skills and procedures you are familiar with to be successful with these new perms.

LESSONS LEARNED

>> A pre-perm analysis of the porosity, elasticity, texture and density of the client's hair will help you choose the right base size and tool size, select the proper perm solution and manage processing time.

- Porosity refers to the ability of the hair to absorb moisture, liquids or chemicals.

- Elasticity is the hair's ability to be stretched and return to its original shape.

- The texture of hair is often categorized as fine, medium or coarse.

- Density refers to the number of hair follicles per square inch.

>> The five-step procedure to ensure predictable results in perming includes distribute, section, wrap, process and neutralize.

- The four main ways to distribute the hair are: away from the face, toward the face, from a side part, and in alternating clockwise and counterclockwise directions.

- Sectioning divides the head into several large sections for control, prior to wrapping a perm.

- The two basic wrapping techniques are overlap (croquignole) and spiral.

- The most common perm tool used is a perm rod. Perm rods are usually cylindrical and straight or concave in shape.

- Processing solution is applied to one rod at a time, to ensure thorough and even penetration of the chemical solution.

- Rinsing stops processing action and removes all of perm solution from hair before neutralizing.

- Neutralizer can be rinsed with the rods in position (for a stronger curl) or after rods are removed and neutralizer is worked through ends; hair must be rinsed carefully and thoroughly.

PERM

111.5

GUEST EXPERIENCE

EXPLORE //

Providing a memorable guest experience goes beyond your technical skills. Can you remember receiving a service in which the *experience* factored heavily into your decision to return as a loyal client?

» INSPIRE //

When you provide
an extraordinary guest
experience, a new client
often becomes a loyal
client. Loyal clients tend to
spend more and tell others
about the experience they have
with you.

ACHIEVE //

Following this lesson on *Perm Guest Experience*, you'll be able to:

» Summarize the service essentials related to perm services

» Provide examples of infection control and safety guidelines for perm services

FOCUS //

PERM GUEST EXPERIENCE

Perm Service Essentials

Perm Infection Control and Safety

111ᶜ.5 |
PERM GUEST EXPERIENCE

It's often the little details, such as attentiveness and good communication, that guests remember when it comes to a perm service experience. These details are significant elements of the overall guest experience. Communicating with your client prior to the actual service helps to clarify expectations and ensure the results you and your client are looking for.

SALON**CONNECTION**

Online Consultation

Many salons today are using information management programs to offer online consultation forms for clients to complete before their scheduled appointments. Clients can upload their own pictures as well as images of desired hairstyles for hair designers to preview. While these systems don't replace the stylist's critical thinking, they can save time during the perm service and allow for you to be better prepared before you speak with your client in person.

PERM SERVICE ESSENTIALS

As you review the Service Essentials, remember the impact of active listening, critical thinking and analysis on the overall success of the service. Pay attention to the following guidelines as you perform the perm service.

CONNECT

>> Meet and greet the client with a firm handshake and pleasant tone of voice.

>> Communicate to build rapport and develop a relationship with the client.

CONSULT

» Help your client fill out a consultation form.

» Analyze your client's wants and needs by asking questions. Determine what type of design the client expects. Identify how much texture is needed. Use photos or a style guide for clear communication.

» Consider your client's lifestyle. Does your client have a busy lifestyle or enough available time to spend styling their hair? Can the client handle a high-maintenance style or is a low-maintenance look required?

» Ask about your client's perming history. Have there been problems with perming in the past? Are there particular details your client can share about the behavior and reactions of their hair?

» Analyze your client's face and body shape, physical features, lifestyle, climate effects, hair and scalp type, condition, prior product usage and results from previous services.

» Assess the facts and thoroughly think through your recommendations.

» Document everything that is important to the successful outcome of this service, as well as future services.

» Have your client sign a release form, which is required by some malpractice insurance companies. It states that the school or salon is not responsible for damages that may occur.

» Explain your recommendations, as well as the price for today's and possible future services.

» Further consult and clarify any communication if your client is hesitant with your recommendations.

» Gain feedback from your client and obtain consent before proceeding with service.

CREATE

» Ensure your client is protected by draping with a plastic cape and towel.

» Always use extreme care when working with chemicals.

» Ensure client comfort throughout the service.

» Pay particular attention to preventing the perm chemicals from dripping onto your client's face and neck and from irritating the scalp.

» Deliver all steps of the perm service to the best of your ability.

» Teach the client how to perform home hair-care maintenance to keep the new waves or curls looking healthy and vibrant.

COMPLETE

» Request specific feedback from your client. Ask questions and look for verbal and nonverbal cues to determine your client's level of satisfaction.

» Recommend products to maintain the healthy condition of your client's hair.

» Prebook – Suggest a future appointment time for your client's next visit.

» Offer sincere appreciation to your client for visiting the school or salon.

» Accompany your client to the reception/payment area or to the door. Send the client off with a warm farewell.

» Complete the client record with accurate information for future services.

CLIENT RECORD/RELEASE FORM

A client release statement helps the school or salon owner avoid retribution as a result of any damages or accidents and may be required as part of some malpractice insurance policies.

>> It is not a legal document.

>> It may not absolve the hairstylist from responsibility for damage that may occur to the client's hair as a result of the chemical service.

CLIENT CHEMICAL PERMANENT RECORD

Date	Wrap	Rod Size	Products	Process Time	Strand Test
				☐ Negative ☐ Positive Remarks:	☐ Good ☐ Poor ☐ Too Tight ☐ Too Loose Remarks:

Description of Hair:

Length	Density	Texture	Porosity	Elasticity	Test Curl Results
• Short	• Light	• Fine	• Average	• Good	• Negative
• Medium	• Medium	• Medium	• Resistant	• Normal	• Positive
• Long	• Heavy	• Coarse	• Extreme Porosity	• Poor	

Medications: _____

Vitamins: _____

Comments: _____

_____

_____

_____

Price of Service: _____

Signature of Student:

_____

Signature of Instructor:

_____

CLIENT CHEMICAL PERMANENT RELEASE FORM

Name: _____   Phone Number: _____

Address: _____   City, State, Postal Code: _____

I request a permanent and I fully understand that this service is to be given by a student of cosmetology at Your Name Beauty School. I hereby express my willingness for a student to do this work. I furthermore understand that I will assume full responsibility thereof.

Your Name Beauty School

Witness: _____   Client Signature: _____

Date: _____   Date: _____

DISCOVERMORE

Many salons are using social media marketing to grow their businesses. Word-of-mouth is still the best form of advertising. After the completion of the service, salon professionals are encouraging their clients to take "selfies" and post them to their social media pages and/or virtual boards, mentioning the hair professional and salon name. Clients are offered incentives for resulting referrals.

COMMUNICATION GUIDELINES

The following chart will help you respond to the most common client cues in a way that encourages client trust, loyalty and open communication.

CLIENT CUE	DESIGNER RESPONSE
"I feel something pulling."	"Please point to the area and I'll make an adjustment. I don't want you to have a pulling sensation anywhere during any part of the perm service. Please let me know if you do feel anything pulling. There, how does that feel?"
"Can't they make these perms smell any better?"	"They do smell much better than they used to. I'm always careful to rinse the solution thoroughly to remove as much of the odor as possible."
"My shirt was ruined the last time I permed my hair."	"We use a special draping method during chemical services. I'll check on the drape throughout the service to make extra sure you and your clothes stay dry. Please let me know if you notice any wetness."
"I feel a tingling around my forehead."	"Let me check the area. I'll blot what might be excess solution and replace the cotton. Please let me know if the tingling feeling continues."
"I feel something wet dripping down my neck."	"Thank you for telling me. Let me change the draping."
"Is it possible to have a hair color and a perm service on the same day?"	"In many cases, yes. I can add shine and depth to your hair with a temporary, semi-permanent or demi-permanent hair color on the same day. And, if you would like your hair slightly lighter, as long as your hair is in good condition, I can use a permanent hair color—if you wait about one week after the perm service. Also, to maintain the integrity of your hair, I don't recommend any color service that requires a lightener (bleach)."
"I love my perm. Is there anything special that I should keep in mind to maintain it?"	"Yes, there are several things you can do to maintain your perm. Here are some things I recommend: 1. Wait about 48 hours before you shampoo and condition your hair. 2. Use leave-in conditioners and avoid using heavy creams that can weigh your hair down. Also, avoid using brushes or combs that will stretch your hair. Instead, use a wide-tooth comb on both wet and dry hair. 3. You can use texturizing creams to define curls, and shine sprays or gloss for a healthy-looking finish. 4. Use a diffuser for a "scrunched" effect, or let your hair air dry for a natural look. 5. Avoid using excessive heat with thermal tools. Instead, set your hair with rollers if you want a more structured finish."

PERM INFECTION CONTROL AND SAFETY

It is your responsibility to protect your client by following infection control and safety guidelines with any and all services you provide.

Cleaning is a process of removing dirt, debris and potential pathogens to aid in slowing the growth of pathogens. Cleaning is performed prior to disinfection procedures.

Disinfection methods kill certain pathogens (bacteria, viruses and fungi) with the exception of spores. Disinfectants are available in varied forms, including concentrate, liquid, spray or wipes that are approved EPA-registered disinfectants available for use in the salon industry. Immersion, and the use of disinfecting spray or wipes are common practices when it comes to disinfecting tools, multi-use supplies and equipment in the salon. Be sure to follow the manufacturer's directions for mixing disinfecting solutions and contact times, if applicable.

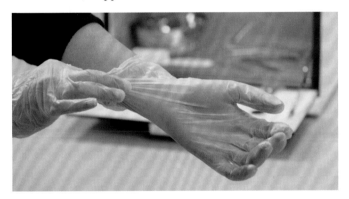

SAFETY PRECAUTIONS

The following is a list of safety precautions that you should always adhere to prior to and during a perm service to protect the client and yourself.

1. Practice infection control guidelines. Wash your hands.

2. Protect yourself. Wear gloves when applying chemical solutions.

3. Protect your client's clothing with proper draping. See "Draping for Chemical Services" section in this lesson.

4. Check the scalp for abrasions or diseases. Do not proceed with perm services if abrasions or diseases are present. See "Scalp Analysis" in this lesson.

5. Determine if your client has experienced an allergic reaction to any other previous perm service prior to beginning the current perm service. Conduct a test curl to help determine how your client's hair will react to a perm.

6. Avoid perming damaged hair that shows breakage. If the hair is dry, brittle or overporous, recondition it first. Cut off damaged hair ends and select a mild perm formula.

7. Never perm hair that has been treated with a sodium hydroxide or a no-lye relaxer. The results could be severe breakage and/or irreversible damage.

8. Analyze your client's hair to determine the correct perm solution to be used. Identify if the hair has been tinted, bleached, highlighted or previously permed.

9. Perform a test for metallic salts if there is a possibility that such a product is on the hair. See "Test for Metallic Salts" later in this lesson.

10. Before the chemical phase of the perm, protect your client's skin by applying barrier/protective cream and cotton around the hairline. Replace the cotton when it becomes saturated. Note that solution-saturated cotton could cause chemical burns if left on the skin.

11. Throw away any opened, unused perm solution or neutralizer. These products can change in strength and effectiveness if they are not used soon after being opened.

12. Follow the manufacturer's directions. Do not dilute or add anything to the solution or the neutralizer unless indicated by the manufacturer's directions.

13. Keep all products out of the eyes and away from the skin as much as possible. If the products come into contact with these areas, rinse immediately and thoroughly with tepid water.

14. If a plastic bag is used during processing, do not allow it to rest on the skin. It should be attached over the cotton strip that is positioned around the hairline.

15. Complete the client record, noting any allergies or adverse reactions the client may have experienced.

DRAPING FOR CHEMICAL SERVICES

Proper draping procedures for chemical services protect the client's clothing, as well as help prevent skin irritations or burns caused by the chemicals you apply. Draping for chemical services is not the same as draping for a shampoo.

DRAPING GUIDELINES FOR A CHEMICAL SERVICE

1. Wash hands.

2. Ask client to remove neck jewelry, earrings and eyeglasses (if applicable); store in a secure place.

3. Turn client's collar under.

4. Place towel around client's neck and fasten plastic shampoo cape over towel; be sure cape covers back of chair. Check with client to be sure that cape is not too tight, yet fits snugly enough to prevent water or solution from dripping onto clothing.

5. Fold edge of towel down over cape and drape second towel over shampoo cape; fasten securely with a clamp.

6. Check before applying chemical solutions and performing rinsing procedures that cape has not fallen inside back of chair.

SCALP ANALYSIS

Since perming involves the use of chemicals, it is important to examine and analyze the condition of your client's scalp before the service in order to ensure client safety.

» The following are guidelines to follow when performing a scalp analysis. Look for any abnormalities on the scalp, such as:
   ▪ Cuts
   ▪ Scratches
   ▪ Sores
   ▪ Abrasions

» If you find any of these irregularities, postpone the perm service until the scalp is healthy again.

» Never apply chemicals over any abnormal scalp condition. To do so could cause chemical burns and scalp problems.

» When the scalp is healthy, you may proceed with the service, provided the hair is structurally competent.

PRELIMINARY TEST CURLS

Preliminary test curls help determine how your client's hair will react to a perm. Take the time to test hair that is bleached, overporous, damaged or has been colored with henna.

1. Shampoo hair once using gentle massage movements and gently towel-dry.

2. Wrap one perm rod in a concealed area (represents the overall condition of hair), following perm directions.

3. Apply protective cream to surrounding area and cover with plastic.

4. Wrap coil of cotton around perm rod to protect surrounding hair from chemicals.

5. Apply perm solution to the wrapped hair; keep the chemicals away from unwrapped hair.

6. Set timer and process according to the manufacturer's directions.

7. Check test curl at least every five minutes.

To check a test curl:

>> Unfasten and carefully unwind curl 1½ to 2 turns of rod; do not let hair loosen or unwind completely from rod

>> Hold thumbs together on back of rod and turn rod back toward head; do not push perm rod toward head

>> If S-shape or pattern is not evident, rewrap rod and continue processing

>> Observe hair carefully and look for overly softened hair

>> When undulation is ready, hair will automatically form a strong, well-defined S-shape or pattern

>> When you achieve a positive test curl, proceed with the rinsing and neutralizing steps

Examine the finished curl. If desired results are achieved, proceed with perm service. Note that this is the same procedure used for testing curls during the actual perm processing time.

Color products that contain metallic salts (refer to the lesson

TEST FOR METALLIC SALTS

on *Nonoxidative Color Products*) form a residue on the hair that interferes with the chemical action of a perm. The results can be uneven curls, distinct discoloration, hair damage or breakage. If you suspect metallic salts are present, perform a "1:20 test," also known as incompatibility test, prior to performing a perm service. To perform the 1:20 test:

>> Mix 1 ounce (30 ml) of 20 volume (6%) peroxide and 20 drops of 28% ammonia in a glass bowl

>> Remove at least 20 strands of hair and immerse in this mixture for 30 minutes

>> Look for any of these possible results:

   ▪ If hair strands lighten slightly, there are no metallic salts present; you may proceed with the perm.

   ▪ If hair strands lighten quickly, hair contains lead– do not perm.

   ▪ If there is no reaction after 30 minutes, hair contains silver–do not perm.

   ▪ If solution begins to boil within a few minutes, giving off an unpleasant odor, and if hair degrades and pulls apart easily, hair contains copper–do not perm.

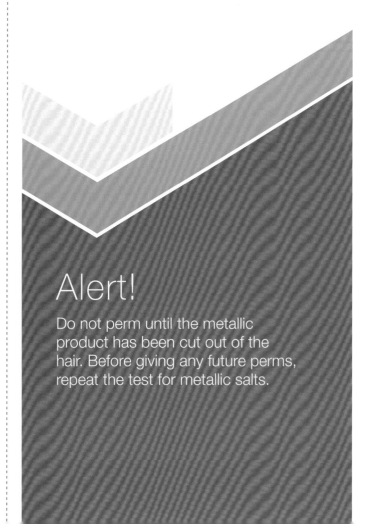

Alert!

Do not perm until the metallic product has been cut out of the hair. Before giving any future perms, repeat the test for metallic salts.

CLEANING AND DISINFECTION GUIDELINES

Keep in mind that only nonporous tools, supplies and equipment can be disinfected. All single-use items must be discarded after each use. Always follow your area's regulatory guidelines.

TOOLS, SUPPLIES AND EQUIPMENT	CLEANING GUIDELINES	DISINFECTION GUIDELINES
Applicator Bottle	» Preclean with soap and water.	» Use an approved EPA-registered disinfectant solution, wipe or spray.
Perm Tools/Rods	» Remove hair and debris. Preclean with soap and water.	» Use an approved EPA-registered disinfectant solution, wipe or spray.
Combs	» Remove hair and debris. Preclean with soap and water.	» Immerse in an approved EPA-registered disinfectant solution.
Plastic Sectioning Clips	» Preclean with soap and water.	» Immerse in an approved EPA-registered disinfectant solution.
Spray Bottle	» Preclean with soap and water.	» Use an approved EPA-registered disinfectant solution, wipe or spray.
Plastic Shampoo Cape	» Remove hair and chemical product from cape. » Wash in washing machine with soap after each use.	» Some regulatory agencies may require use of an approved EPA-registered disinfectant.
Perm Bib/Neutralizing Cape	» Remove hair and chemical product from cape. » Wash in washing machine with soap after each use.	» Some regulatory agencies may require use of an approved EPA-registered disinfectant.
Towels	» Remove hair from towels. » Wash in washing machine with soap after each use.	» Some regulatory agencies may require use of an approved EPA-registered disinfectant.

Store disinfected tools and multi-use supplies in a clean, dry, covered container or cabinet.

 **Alert!** If tools, multi-use supplies or equipment have come in contact with blood or body fluids, the following disinfection procedures must take place:

 Use an approved EPA-registered hospital disinfectant according to manufacturer's directions and as required by your area's regulatory agency.

CARE AND SAFETY

Follow infection control procedures for personal care and client safety guidelines before and during the perm service to ensure your safety and the client's, while also contributing to the salon care.

Personal Care		Client Care Prior to the Service	
Refer to your area's regulatory agency for proper mixing/handling of disinfectant solutions.		Perform an incompatibility test for metallic salts if there is a possibility that such a product is on the hair.	
Check that your personal standards of health and hygiene minimize the spread of infection.	Minimize fatigue by maintaining good posture during the service.	Protect the client's skin and clothing from chemicals by draping them with a towel for a perm service.	Conduct a test curl to help determine how your client's hair will react to a perm.
Wash hands and dry thoroughly with a single-use towel.	Ensure your appearance meets accepted industry and organizational requirements.	Be sure the cape stays in place and the client's arms are underneath the cape.	Avoid perming damaged hair that shows breakage. If the hair is dry, brittle or overporous, recondition it first. Cut off damaged hair ends and select a milder perm lotion. If necessary, postpone the service until the hair is in good enough condition.
Disinfect workstation.		Check the scalp for any diseases or disorders. If any are evident, refer client to a physician; do not proceed with the service.	Analyze your client's hair to determine the correct perm lotion to use. Identify if the hair has been previously chemically treated.
Clean and disinfect tools appropriately.		Do not proceed with the service if there are any cuts or irritations on the client's scalp.	Determine if your client has experienced an allergic reaction to any other previous perm service prior to beginning the current perm service.
Wear protective single-use or multi-use gloves when applying chemical solutions.		If any tools are dropped on the floor, pick them up, then clean and disinfect.	Never perm hair that has been treated with sodium hydroxide or a no-lye relaxer.

Client Care During the Service

If a plastic bag is used during the process, do not allow it to rest on the skin. It should be attached over the cotton strip/barrier cream that is positioned around the hairline.

Shampoo as recommended by perm manufacturer.	Monitor the perm service and perform a test curl as needed to check for curl development.
Follow manufacturer's directions. Do not dilute or add anything to the solution or the neutralizer unless indicated by the manufacturer's directions.	Check in and ask client about any scalp sensitivity or irritations.
Protect the client's skin by applying protective barrier cream and cotton strip around the hairline and ears. Replace the cotton strip when it becomes saturated.	Be sure the cape stays in place and the client's arms are underneath the cape.
Do not permit the product to come in contact with the eyes. If it does, rinse the eyes immediately with tepid water.	

Salon Care

Ensure electrical cords are properly positioned to avoid accidental falls.

Follow your area's health and safety guidelines, including cleaning and disinfecting guidelines.	Discard any opened, unused perm solution or neutralizer once the service is complete (down the sink with plenty of water). These products can change in strength and effectiveness if they are not used soon after being opened.
Ensure equipment, including the salon chair, is clean and disinfected.	Refer to SDS (Safety Data Sheets).
Promote a professional image by ensuring your workstation is clean and tidy throughout the service.	Update the client record, noting the perm product, perm rods, pattern, processing time and any sensitivities experienced.
Disinfect all tools after each use. Always use disinfected applicator bottles, brushes and combs for each client.	Clean/mop water spillage to avoid accidental falls.

Following the four Service Essentials and proper infection control and safety guidelines will help you provide an exceptional guest experience—which gives you the opportunity for prebooking your client's return for perm services.

LESSONS LEARNED

The service essentials related to a perm service can be summarized as follows:

>> Connect – Meet and greet clients and communicate to build rapport.

>> Consult – Ask questions to discover client needs; analyze client's face and body shape, physical features, hair and scalp; explain recommended solutions and gain feedback for consent to move forward.

>> Create – Ensure client safety and comfort; stay focused to deliver the best service; explain process and products to your client; teach the client at-home care maintenance.

>> Complete – Request specific feedback; recommend home-care products; suggest future appointment times; update client record.

Infection control and safety guidelines must be followed throughout a perm service to ensure your safety and the safety of the clients and the salon. Disinfectants are available in varied forms, including concentrate, liquid, spray or wipes that have EPA approval for use in the salon industry. Be guided by your area's regulatory agency for proper cleaning and disinfection guidelines.

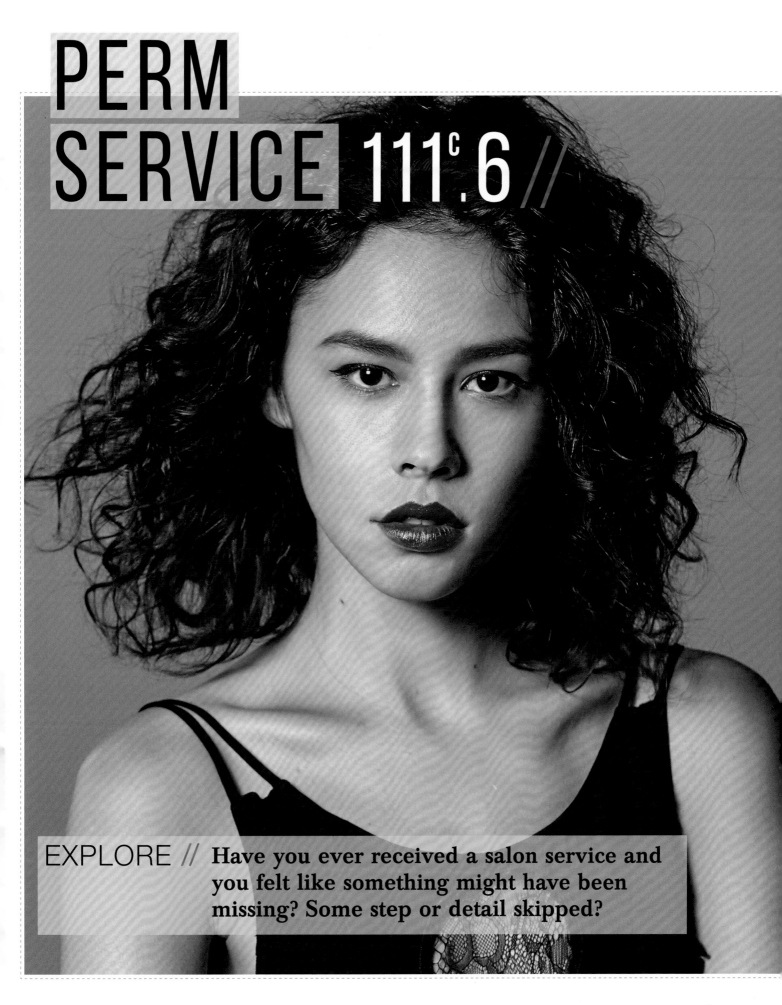

PERM
SERVICE 111ᶜ.6 //

EXPLORE // Have you ever received a salon service and you felt like something might have been missing? Some step or detail skipped?

INSPIRE //

Using proper perm procedures before, during and after the perm service ensures beautiful and reliable perm results—and clients who rebook!

ACHIEVE //

Following this lesson on *Perm Service*, you'll be able to:

>> Provide examples of procedural guidelines to follow when performing a perm service

>> Describe the three areas of a perm service

>> Restate solutions to common perm problems

FOCUS //

PERM SERVICE

Perm Client Guidelines

Perm Service Overview

Perm Problems and Solutions

Perm Rubric

111°.6 | PERM SERVICE

This lesson is a culmination of everything you've learned about perm theory, tools, skills and guest experience; it's where you apply your knowledge, before, during and after the perm service to ensure client safety and satisfaction.

PERM CLIENT GUIDELINES

To ensure your client's comfort and safety during the perm service, keep the following guidelines in mind when performing the perm procedures.

DISTRIBUTE		» Face client toward mirror, and describe why you are distributing the hair in the direction selected. » Consider hairline growth patterns, such as a widow's peak.
SECTION		» Explain to client that you are using a sectioning pattern that is specifically designed to achieve desired results, e.g., taking growth patterns into consideration. » Consider natural growth patterns and adjust sections if needed.
WRAP		» Turn client chair to accommodate easy access to end papers and perm rods. » Organize end papers and rods to work more efficiently and save client time, e.g., utilize end paper dispenser, detangle rods for easy access. » Check with client to be sure hair is not being pulled uncomfortably tight. » Ensure that the comb you are using does not cause scalp abrasions. » Consider client comfort when positioning and securing rods around the hairline.
PROCESS	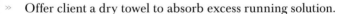	» Maintain client comfort by ensuring cape is on outside-back of chair and draping is secure. » Position cotton around entire hairline to prevent product from dripping into client's eyes and ears, and/or onto clothing. » Offer client a dry towel to absorb excess running solution. » Replace cotton and draping as they become overly wet. » Inform client of the approximate processing time. » Offer beverage or reading material to client. » Ensure client's neck is comfortable during rinsing procedures. » Ask client if water temperature is comfortable. » Position your hand to shield client's face and ears while rinsing.
NEUTRALIZE		» Maintain client comfort by ensuring the cape is on the outside of the back of the chair, cotton is positioned appropriately and draping is secure. » Give information regarding the next step. » Ensure water temperature is comfortable for client while rinsing. » Remove stabilizers and perm tools gently as hair may be caught in tools. » Give client a dry towel so they can dab any excess water from face and/or neck.

PERM SERVICE OVERVIEW

The Perm Service Overview identifies the three areas of all perm services:

>> The Perm Preparation provides a brief overview of the steps to follow before you actually begin the perm service.

>> The Perm Procedure provides an overview of the perm procedures that you will use during the perm service to ensure predictable results.

>> The Perm Completion provides an overview of the steps to follow after performing the perm service to ensure guest satisfaction.

SALON**CONNECTION**

Expand Your Tool Kit

As the new textured looks gain in popularity, you'll need to hone your skills and stay up-to-date with new perm innovations and techniques. In this service-oriented industry, the bar is set high, and clients expect you to create their new textured look while providing an excellent service experience. Accomplishing this will set you apart from other salon professionals.

SERVICE ESSENTIALS: THE FOUR Cs

1. **CONNECT**
   Establishes rapport and builds credibility with each client

2. **CONSULT**
   Analyzes client wants and needs, visualizes the end result, organizes the plan for follow-through and obtains client consent

3. **CREATE**
   Produces functional, predictable and pleasing results

4. **COMPLETE**
   Reviews the service experience and client satisfaction, offers product recommendations, expresses appreciation and provides follow-up

DISCOVER**MORE**

Product companies are capitalizing on the texture industry and are continuously creating and/or improving products accompanied with specialized formulations and techniques. Stay current on what's new: Subscribe to hair and fashion publications, sign up for texture classes offered at shows, salons and educational institutions. Always continue to invest in your craft—the return on your investment is success!

PERM SERVICE OVERVIEW

PERM PREPARATION	» Clean and disinfect workstation.
	» Arrange perm design essentials, including perm tools, rods, stabilizers, end papers, sectioning clips, tail comb, plastic cap, gloves, cotton, perm solution and neutralizer.
	» Wash hands.
	» Perform analysis of hair and scalp.
	» Ask client to remove jewelry, and store in a secure place.
PERM PROCEDURE	» Drape client for a chemical service.
	» Shampoo hair lightly without scalp massage.
	» Perform preliminary test curl.
	» Perform perm procedures to achieve desired results:
	1. **Distribute** the hair in the direction the hair will be worn.
	2. **Section** the hair according to the desired wrapping pattern.
	3. **Wrap** using a 1x half-off base control or other base control, depending on desired result.
	▪ Secure perm tools with stabilizers or picks.
	▪ Place barrier cream and cotton along hairline.
	4. **Apply** processing solution; process according to manufacturer's directions.
	▪ Take test curls, if needed.
	5. **Neutralize** according to manufacturer's directions.
	▪ Rinse processing solution and towel-blot each perm tool.
	▪ Apply neutralizer.
	▪ Remove perm tools and rinse neutralizer.
PERM COMPLETION	» Reinforce client's satisfaction with the overall salon experience.
	» Make professional product recommendations.
	» Prebook client's next appointment.
	» End guest's visit with a warm and personal goodbye.
	» Discard single-use supplies, disinfect tools and multi-use supplies, disinfect workstation and arrange in proper order.
	» Wash your hands.
	» Complete client record.

PERM PROBLEMS AND SOLUTIONS

The following section alerts you to some problems that may occur with perms, along with their possible causes and solutions.

WEAK OR LIMP CURL

Cause: Underprocessing; perm solution not left on the hair long enough

Solution: Follow manufacturer's self-timing recommendations; use a timer for accuracy; take accurate test curls.

Cause: Using perm rods that are too large for desired curl

Solution: Make sure hair completes at least 2½ revolutions around the perm rod, or reduce rod diameter.

Cause: Hair is wrapped too loosely around perm rod

Solution: Wrap with smooth, even tension; acid perms generally require more tension than alkaline perms; always read and follow manufacturer's directions.

Cause: Incorrect choice of perm product

Solution: Analyze your client's hair, and match your findings to the perm performance description listed by the manufacturer.

UNEVEN CURL

Cause: Inconsistent application of perm solution and/or neutralizer

Solution: Apply chemicals in a systematic method to avoid missing any perm rods.

Cause: Incomplete rinsing or blotting

Solution: Be consistent; rinse and blot all rods thoroughly.

Cause: Too much hair wrapped on perm rods or hair is not evenly distributed on rod

Solution: Base sizes equal to the diameter of the rod will give you the most consistent curl pattern; avoid bunching hair, and wrap it as smoothly as possible around rods.

FRIZZINESS

Cause: Overprocessing; perm solution left on the hair too long; may look curly when wet but frizzy when dry

Solution: Take frequent test curls; use timer to accurately track time.

Cause: Hair is stretched or manipulated too much after perm when thermal designing

Solution: Use finishing products designed to define curl patterns; dry with warm heat using little tension on the hair.

BREAKAGE OR DRYNESS

Cause: Hair is wrapped on perm rods with too much tension

Solution: Avoid excessive stretching; moderate tension is advisable.

Cause: Hair is too fragile for perming

Solution: Perform thorough pre-perm analysis of hair to determine if perming is advisable; perform preliminary test curl if in doubt.

Cause: Perm rod band places pressure on hair during processing

Solution: Lift band off hair by placing picks under it.

SKIN IRRITATION

Cause: Cotton or neck towel is allowed to remain on skin after it was saturated with perm solution

Solution: Replace with fresh cotton or towel, as needed; do not allow solution-soaked cotton to remain on skin, especially under plastic cap.

UNPLEASANT ODOR AFTER PERMING

Cause: Insufficient rinsing of perm solution before neutralizing

Solution: Rinse hair for a full 5 minutes or longer; check for proper rinsing by smelling hair; you should not smell perm; rinse more carefully when using acid or low/no thio perms, since they take longer to remove from hair.

HAIR LIGHTENS AFTER PERM SERVICE

Cause: Many neutralizers contain hydrogen peroxide, which will lighten the hair slightly; lightening effect is more apparent on porous hair

Solution: Apply a temporary color to deposit missing tones; book hair color appointment, if needed, one week or more after perm; follow manufacturer's directions for same-day perm and color services.

PERM DID NOT LAST AS LONG AS EXPECTED

Cause: Hair not in proper condition before perm service

Solution: Recondition weak hair before perming.

Cause: Incomplete neutralization; insufficient blotting after rinsing perm solution, which dilutes neutralizer

Solution: Remove excess water by blotting the entire head first and then each perm rod before applying neutralizer.

PERM RUBRIC

A performance rubric is a document that identifies defined criteria at which levels of performance can be measured objectively. The Perm Rubric is an example that your instructor might choose to use for scoring. The Perm Rubric is divided into three main areas—Preparation, Procedure and Completion. Each area is further divided into step-by-step procedures that will ensure client safety and satisfaction.

PERM RUBRIC

Allotted Time: 1 Hour, 30 Minutes

Student Name: _____ ID Number: _____

Instructor: _____ Date: _____ Start Time: _____ End Time: _____

PERM (Live Model) – *Each scoring item is marked with either a "Yes" or "No." Each "Yes" counts for one point. Total number of points attainable is 36.*

CRITERIA	YES	NO	INSTRUCTOR ASSESSMENT
PREPARATION: *Did student...*			
1. Set up workstation with properly labeled supplies?	☐	☐	
2. Place disinfected tools and supplies at a visibly clean workstation?	☐	☐	
3. Wash hands?	☐	☐	
Connect: Did student...			
4. Meet and greet client with a welcoming smile and pleasant tone of voice?	☐	☐	
5. Communicate to build rapport and develop a relationship with client?	☐	☐	
6. Refer to client by name throughout service?	☐	☐	
Consult: Did student...			
7. Ask questions to discover client's wants and needs?	☐	☐	
8. Analyze client's hair and scalp and check for any contraindications?	☐	☐	
9. Gain feedback and consent from client before proceeding?	☐	☐	
PROCEDURE: *Did student...*			
10. Properly drape client and prepare for service?	☐	☐	
11. Ensure client protection and comfort by maintaining cape on outside of chair at all times?	☐	☐	
12. Carry out appropriate shampoo and condition procedures when applicable?	☐	☐	
13. Use products and supplies economically?	☐	☐	
Create: Did student...			
14. Distribute and section the hair appropriately for perm pattern?	☐	☐	
15. Use correct wrapping techniques to include partings, end papers and base controls?	☐	☐	
16. Use correct securing technique?	☐	☐	
17. Prepare perm products correctly?	☐	☐	
18. Apply barrier cream and cotton strip properly to protect skin?	☐	☐	
19. Apply perm solution accurately to each rod, saturating hair?	☐	☐	
20. Apply plastic cap and/or heat according to manufacturer's directions?	☐	☐	
21. Process perm solution according to manufacturer's directions?	☐	☐	
22. Perform test curl to ensure proper curl development?	☐	☐	
23. Rinse thoroughly to remove perm solution from hair and towel-blot hair?	☐	☐	
24. Apply and process neutralizer according to manufacturer's directions?	☐	☐	
25. Rinse thoroughly to remove neutralizer from the hair and towel-blot hair?	☐	☐	
26. Teach client to use products to maintain the appearance and condition of the hair?	☐	☐	
27. Practice infection control procedures and safety guidelines throughout service?	☐	☐	
COMPLETION (Complete): *Did student...*			
28. Ask questions and look for verbal and nonverbal cues to determine client's level of satisfaction?	☐	☐	
29. Make professional product recommendations?	☐	☐	
30. Ask client to make a future appointment?	☐	☐	
31. End guest's visit with a warm and personal goodbye?	☐	☐	
32. Discard single-use supplies?	☐	☐	
33. Disinfect tools and multi-use supplies; disinfect workstation and arrange in proper order?	☐	☐	
34. Complete service within scheduled time?	☐	☐	
35. Complete client record?	☐	☐	
36. Wash hands following service?	☐	☐	

COMMENTS: _____ TOTAL POINTS = _____ ÷ 36 = _____ %

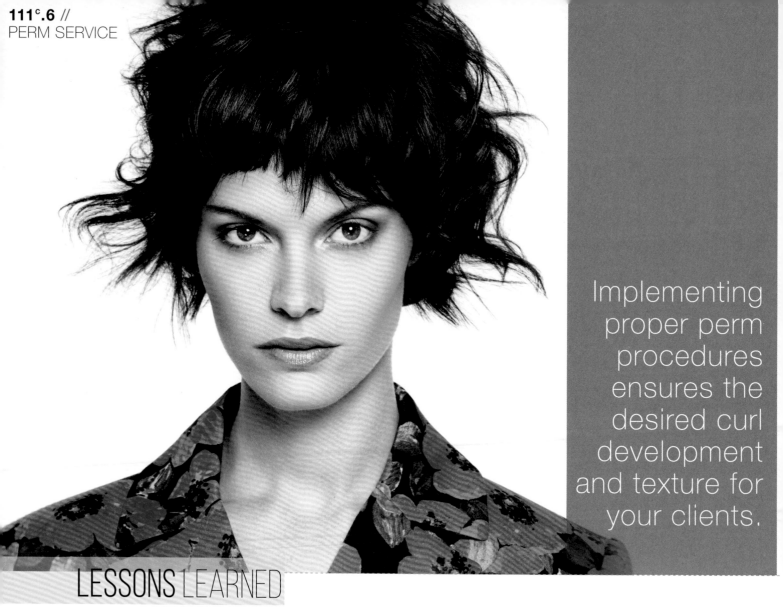

Implementing proper perm procedures ensures the desired curl development and texture for your clients.

LESSONS LEARNED

Perm client guidelines to follow to ensure comfort and satisfaction include:

» Considering natural growth patterns and adjusting distribution and sectioning, if needed

» Turning client chair to accommodate easy access to end papers and perm rods

» Maintaining client comfort by ensuring cape is on the outside-back of the chair and draping is secure; cotton is positioned and replaced, as needed

The Perm Service Overview provides an outline of the steps to follow before, during and after a perm service to ensure client satisfaction. The three areas of a perm service include the Preparation, Procedure and Completion:

» Preparation – Includes setting up the workstation with disinfected rods and implements; connecting and consulting with the client

» Procedure – Includes ensuring client safety, properly draping the client, shampooing the client's hair and conditioning, if appropriate; performing the physical and chemical phases of the perm service, including rinsing of all chemical products

» Completion – Includes infection control and safety procedures, such as discarding non-reusable materials, arranging/disinfecting workstation, determining client's level of satisfaction, recommending products, asking client to make a future appointment, ending guest's visit with a warm and personal goodbye and completing the client record

The Perm Problems and Solutions chart alerts you to some problems that may occur with perms, along with their possible causes and solutions—so you might avoid these problems.

RECTANGLE
PERM PATTERN

EXPLORE

What similarities can you see between a railroad track and the rectangle pattern?

INSPIRE

Practicality and versatility make the rectangle wrap a good choice for many clients. The rectangle pattern is one of the quickest wraps to apply—which will help you stay on schedule in the salon.

ACHIEVE

Following this *Rectangle Perm Pattern Workshop*, you'll be able to:

>> Identify the perm procedures related to the rectangle pattern

>> Identify the appropriate length rods to adapt to the width of each shape in the rectangle perm pattern

>> Create a repetition of curl on uniformly layered lengths using 1x, half-off base control throughout

A repetition of curl texture on uniformly layered lengths moves away from the face at the forehead and down at the sides.

A center rectangle extends from the front hairline to the nape. The sides are divided into two sections. The hair is wrapped to move away from the face at the front and downward at the sides.

PERM PROCEDURES

1. DISTRIBUTE

2. SECTION

3. WRAP

4. PROCESS

5. NEUTRALIZE

DESIGN DECISIONS CHART

RECTANGLE PERM PATTERN

Draw or fill in the boxes with the appropriate answers.

DESIGN DECISIONS

EXISTING TEXTURE

☐ ☐ ☐ ☐

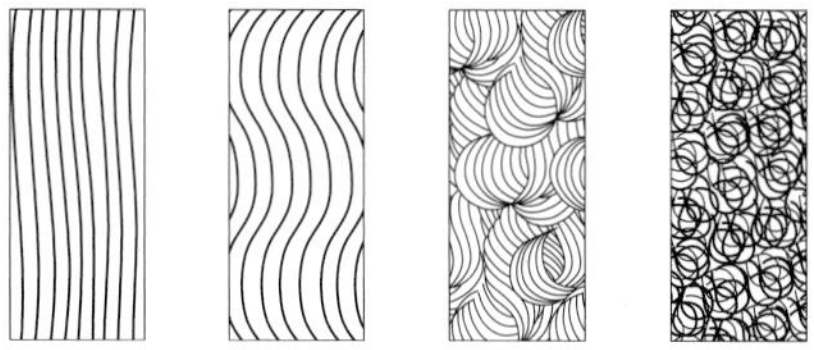

DESIRED TEXTURE

☐ ☐ ☐ ☐

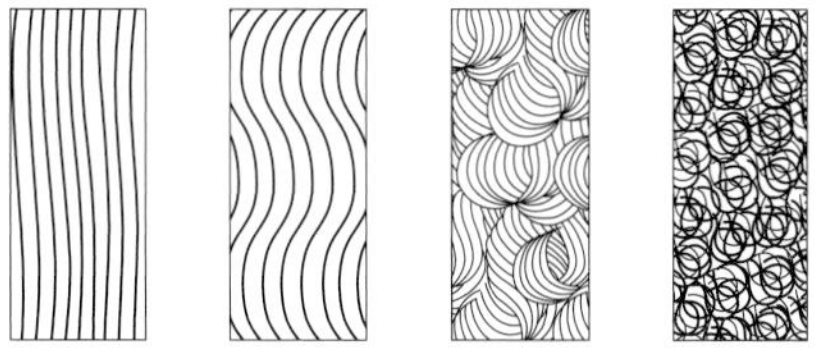

TEXTURE PLACEMENT

STRAND

☐ ☐ ☐

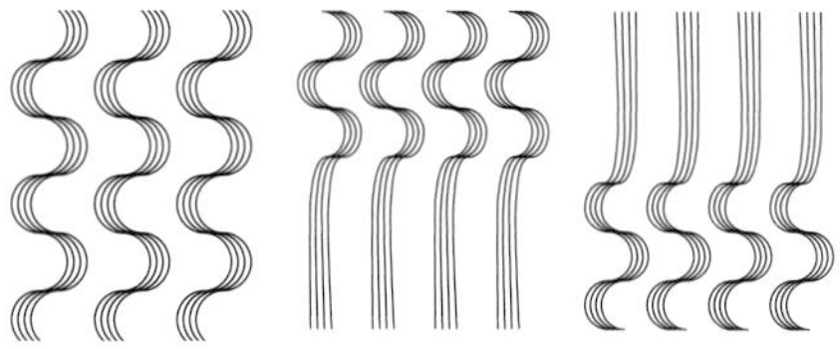

DESIGN PRINCIPLES

☐ ☐ ☐ ☐ ☐ ☐

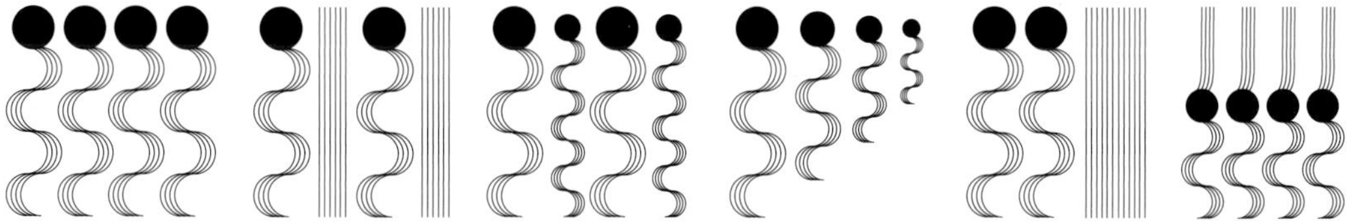

TOOL DIAMETER CHOICES

☐ ☐ ☐

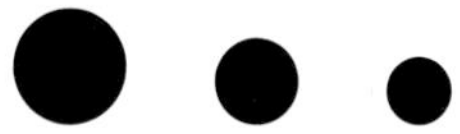

WRAPPING PATTERN/DIRECTION

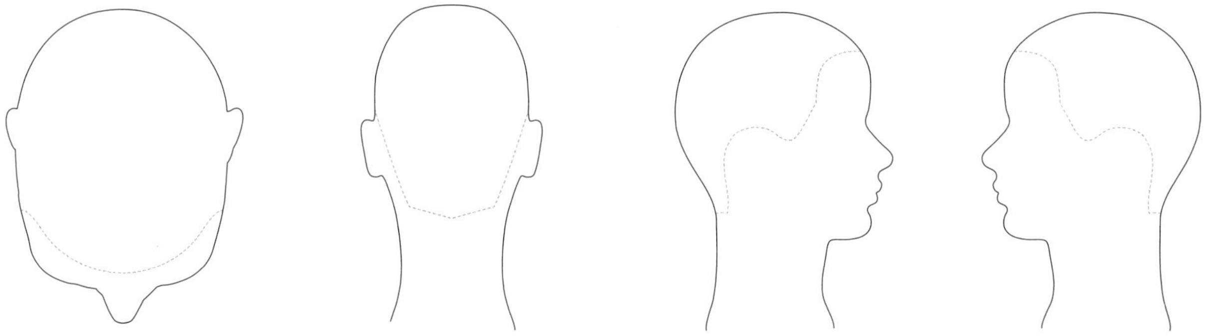

TOOL/PRODUCT CHOICE

____

____

____

Instructor Signature ______________________________ **Date** ______________

PERFORMANCE GUIDE
RECTANGLE PERM PATTERN

View the video, complete the Design Decisions chart, then perform this workshop. Complete the self-check as you progress through the workshop.

20 mins
Suggested
Salon Speed

PREPARATION	✔

>> Assemble tools and products
>> Set up workstation
>> Shampoo hair

☐

DISTRIBUTE/SECTION

1. **Section center rectangle:**

>> Distribute hair away from face
>> Determine section width with length of medium rod
>> Section with tail comb
>> Use shorter rod to measure and taper rectangle at nape

☐

2. **Measure and section front rectangle on either side:**

>> Longer rod
>> Section front of each side from back

☐

3. **Wrap front of center rectangle:**

>> 1x rectangle base at front hairline
>> Measure with diameter of rod
>> Distribute and project 90° from center of base
>> Bookend end-paper technique
>> Overlap wrapping technique
>> Position rod half-off base
>> Fasten band across rod
>> Temporarily position stabilizer or pick toward face

4. **Wrap center rectangle through crown:**

>> Continue 1x bases
>> Position picks or stabilizers in direction of wrap
>> Maintain 90° projection from center of each base
>> Position each rod half-off base

5. **Wrap center rectangle through nape:**

>> Switch to shorter rods used to measure

WRAP – SIDES ✔

6. **The sections behind each ear will be wrapped using:**
   - ›› Horizontal partings
   - ›› Bookend end-paper technique
   - ›› Overlap wrapping technique
   - ›› 1x, half-off base

7. **Wrap left section behind ear:**
   - ›› Start at top with appropriate length rod
   - ›› Work to bottom
   - ›› Adapt rod length to width of section
   - ›› Position stabilizers or picks as needed

8. **Wrap left side:**
   - ›› Work from top to bottom
   - ›› Begin with longer rod used to measure section
   - ›› Adapt rod length to width of section
   - ›› Repeat on opposite side

9. **Position stabilizers or picks:**
   - ›› Check entire head to ensure each rod is half-off base
   - ›› Make sure rods are properly secured

PROCESS/NEUTRALIZE ✔

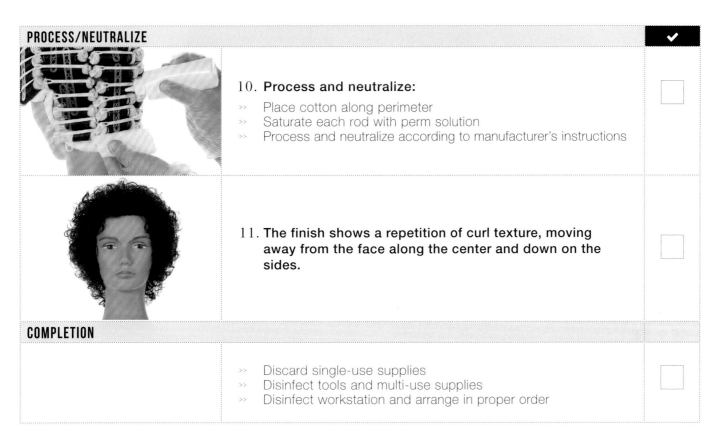

10. **Process and neutralize:**
   >> Place cotton along perimeter
   >> Saturate each rod with perm solution
   >> Process and neutralize according to manufacturer's instructions

11. **The finish shows a repetition of curl texture, moving away from the face along the center and down on the sides.**

COMPLETION

   >> Discard single-use supplies
   >> Disinfect tools and multi-use supplies
   >> Disinfect workstation and arrange in proper order

20 mins
Suggested
Salon Speed

My Speed
_____
_____
_____

INSTRUCTIONS:
Record your time in comparison with the suggested salon speed. Then, list here how you could improve your performance.

_____
_____
_____
_____
_____

VARIATION

A variation on the rectangle pattern wrap is available online. In this double-rod variation, two rod diameters are used within single bases to create a natural-looking combination of curl textures on the longest lengths of a solid form.

CONTOUR
PERM PATTERN

EXPLORE

Have you ever looked at someone with beautiful curls and wondered, "Is that their natural curl or is it a perm?"

INSPIRE

With consistent curls that echo the curve of the head and move away from the face, the contour perm pattern could become one of your "go-to" wraps in the salon.

ACHIEVE

Following this *Contour Perm Pattern Workshop*, you'll be able to:

>> Identify the perm procedures related to the contour pattern

>> Identify the appropriate length rods to adapt to the width of each shape in the contour pattern

>> Create a repetition of curl moving away from the face using 1x, half-off base control

A repetition of curl texture moves away from the face on uniformly layered lengths.

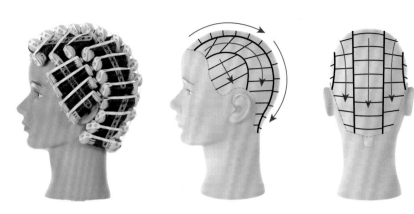

A center rectangle extends from the front hairline to the nape, becoming slightly narrower in the nape. Sections on either side follow the contours of the head, and the sides are wrapped diagonally. The hair is wrapped to move away from the face.

PERM PROCEDURES

1. DISTRIBUTE

2. SECTION

3. WRAP

4. PROCESS

5. NEUTRALIZE

DESIGN DECISIONS CHART

CONTOUR PERM PATTERN

Draw or fill in the boxes with the appropriate answers.

DESIGN DECISIONS

EXISTING TEXTURE

DESIRED TEXTURE

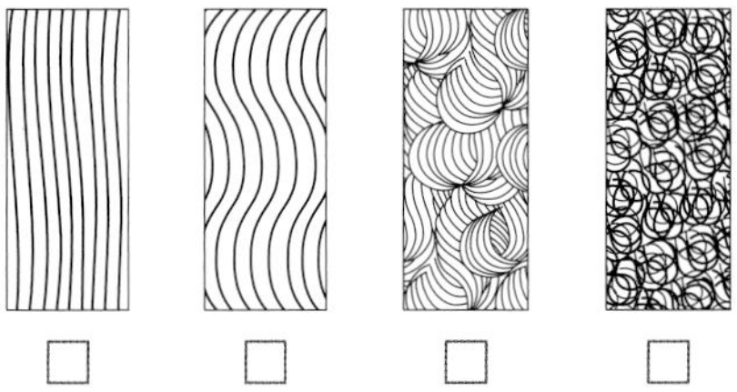

TEXTURE PLACEMENT

STRAND

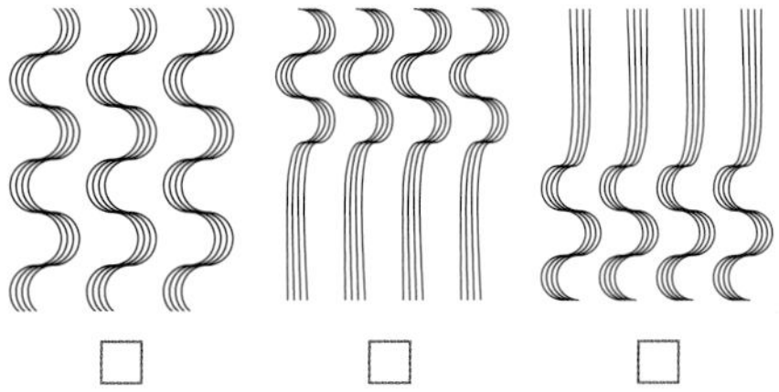

DESIGN PRINCIPLES

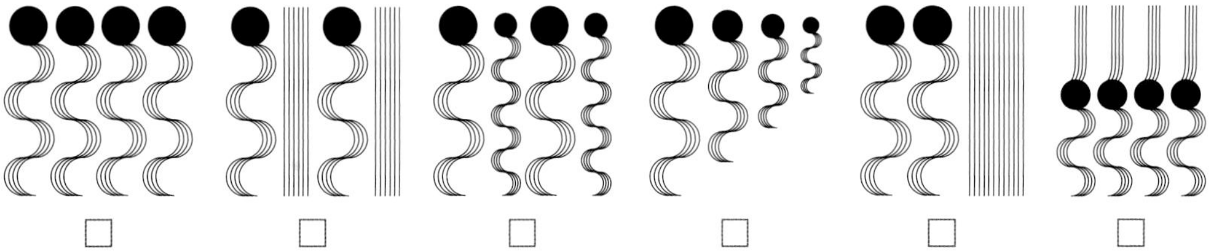

TOOL DIAMETER CHOICES

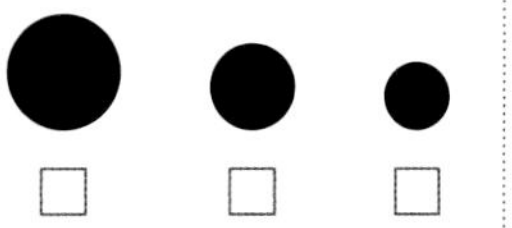

WRAPPING PATTERN/DIRECTION

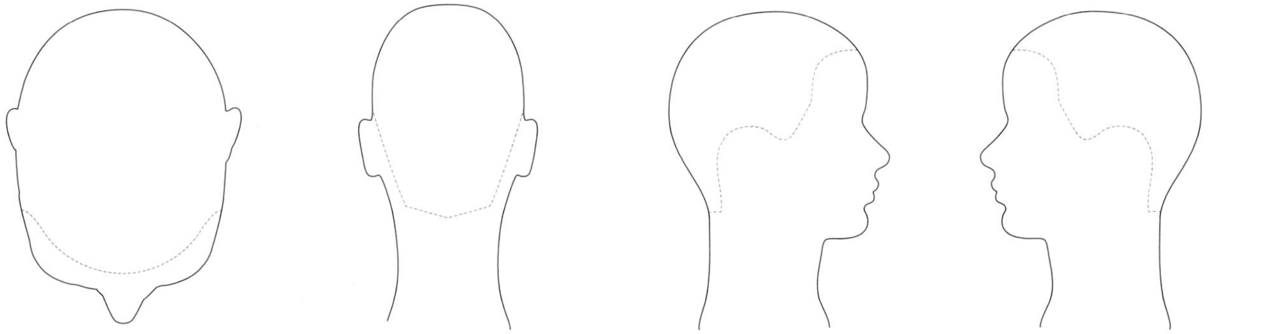

TOOL/PRODUCT CHOICE

_____

_____

_____

Instructor Signature _____ **Date** _____

CONTOUR PERM PATTERN

View the video, complete the Design Decisions chart, then perform
this workshop. Complete the self-check as you progress through
the workshop.

20 mins
Suggested
Salon Speed

PREPARATION		✔
	>> Assemble tools and products >> Set up workstation >> Shampoo hair	☐

DISTRIBUTE/SECTION – CENTER RECTANGLE		
	1. Section center rectangle: >> Distribute hair away from face >> Determine section width with medium-length rod >> Section with tail comb	☐
	2. Measure and section back of rectangle: >> Use shorter tool to adapt to narrow shape in nape	☐

WRAP – CENTER RECTANGLE		
	3. Begin wrapping at front hairline: >> 1x rectangle base >> Measure with diameter of rod >> Distribute and project 90° from center of base >> Bookend end-paper technique >> Overlap wrapping technique >> Position rod half-off base >> Fasten band across rod >> Position pick or stabilizer temporarily toward face	☐

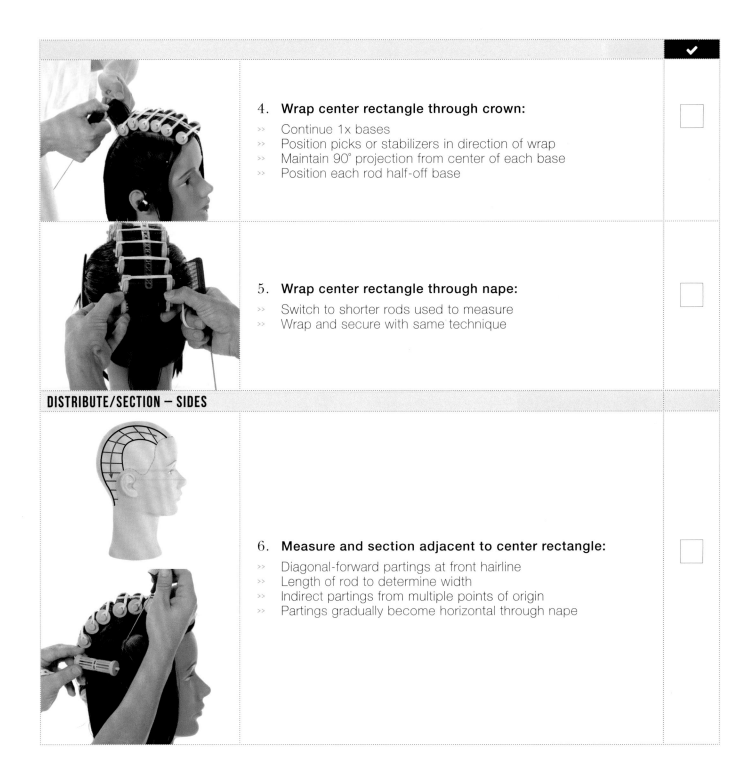

4. **Wrap center rectangle through crown:**
 >> Continue 1x bases
 >> Position picks or stabilizers in direction of wrap
 >> Maintain 90° projection from center of each base
 >> Position each rod half-off base

5. **Wrap center rectangle through nape:**
 >> Switch to shorter rods used to measure
 >> Wrap and secure with same technique

DISTRIBUTE/SECTION – SIDES

6. **Measure and section adjacent to center rectangle:**
 >> Diagonal-forward partings at front hairline
 >> Length of rod to determine width
 >> Indirect partings from multiple points of origin
 >> Partings gradually become horizontal through nape

7. **Wrap section adjacent to center rectangle starting at front hairline:**
   - >> 1x diagonal-forward bases
   - >> 90° projection
   - >> Bookend end-paper technique
   - >> Overlap wrapping technique
   - >> Position rod half-off base, parallel to bottom parting
   - >> Fasten band across rod

8. **Change to horizontal partings and tool position as shape contours head.**

9. **Wrap remaining shape:**
   - >> Diagonal-forward partings
   - >> Adapt rod length to accommodate hairline
   - >> Secure with stabilizer or picks

10. **Repeat on opposite side.**

PROCESS/NEUTRALIZE ✔

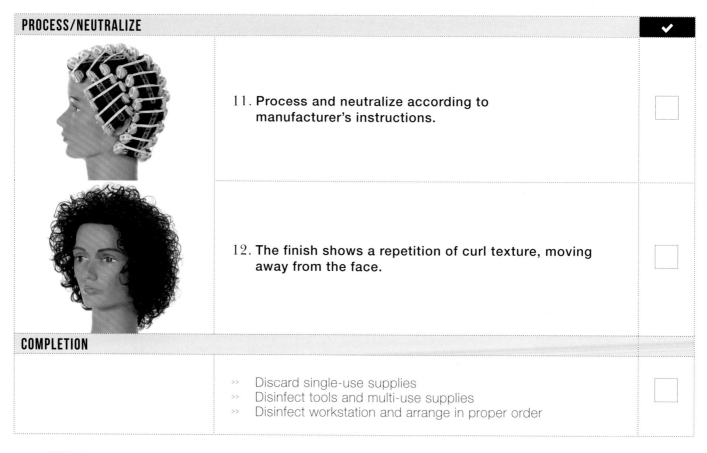

11. Process and neutralize according to manufacturer's instructions.

12. The finish shows a repetition of curl texture, moving away from the face.

COMPLETION

>> Discard single-use supplies
>> Disinfect tools and multi-use supplies
>> Disinfect workstation and arrange in proper order

20 mins
Suggested Salon Speed

My Speed
_____
_____
_____

INSTRUCTIONS:

Record your time in comparison with the suggested salon speed. Then, list here how you could improve your performance.

_____
_____
_____
_____
_____

VARIATION – CONTOUR WRAP

A variation on the contour wrap is available online. In this variation, an alternation of rod diameters is used to create natural-looking texture on an increase-layered form.

BRICKLAY PERM PATTERN
OVERLAP

How might you use the bricklay pattern while doing a hair design? Does this pattern serve the same purpose in a perm design?

INSPIRE

Design consistent curls, echoing the curve of the head, while avoiding any splits and creating a natural look.

ACHIEVE

Following this *Bricklay Perm Pattern – Overlap Workshop*, you'll be able to:

>> Identify the perm procedures related to the bricklay pattern

>> Identify the appropriate length rods to adapt to the shape of the head

>> Wrap a bricklay pattern using the one-two method

>> Create a repetition of curl, moving away from the face, with no visible splits using 1x, half-off base control throughout

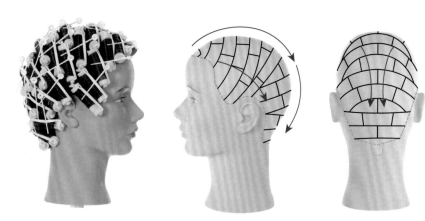

A repetition of curl texture moves away from the face on uniformly layered lengths.

Repetitious curl texture is created in a bricklay pattern, using the one-two method with a consistent tool diameter and half-off base control throughout. Rectangular, trapezoidal and triangular bases are used to accommodate the curves of the head.

PERM PROCEDURES

1. DISTRIBUTE

2. SECTION

N/A

3. WRAP

4. PROCESS

5. NEUTRALIZE

DESIGN DECISIONS CHART

BRICKLAY PERM PATTERN OVERLAP

Draw or fill in the boxes with the appropriate answers.

DESIGN DECISIONS

EXISTING TEXTURE

☐ ☐ ☐ ☐

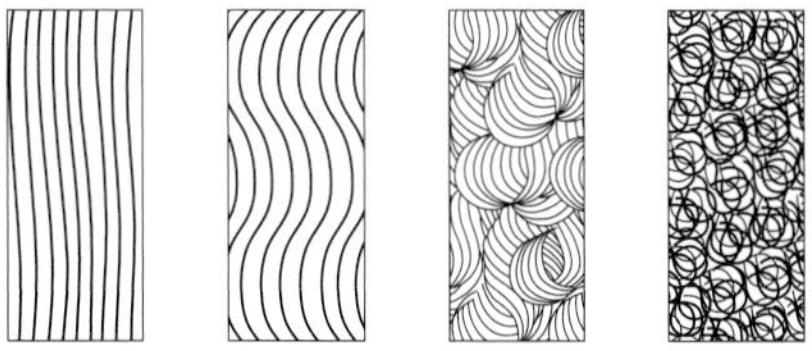

DESIRED TEXTURE

☐ ☐ ☐ ☐

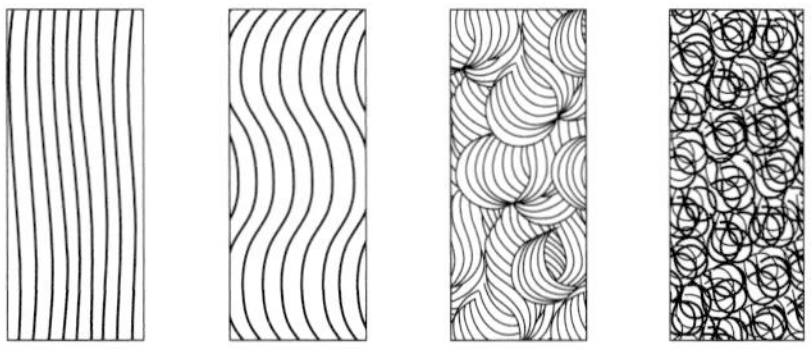

TEXTURE PLACEMENT

STRAND

☐ ☐ ☐

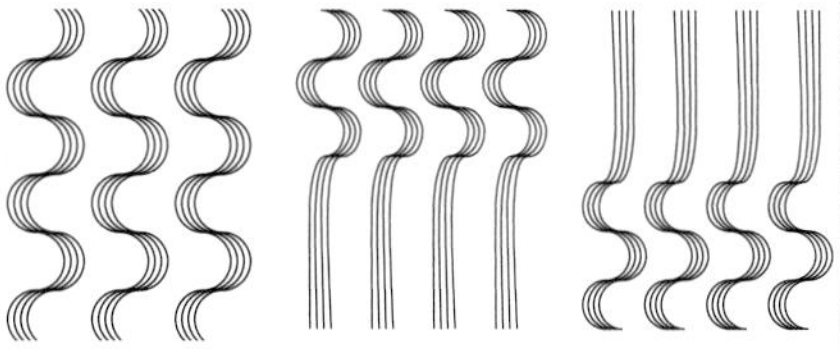

DESIGN PRINCIPLES

☐ ☐ ☐ ☐ ☐ ☐

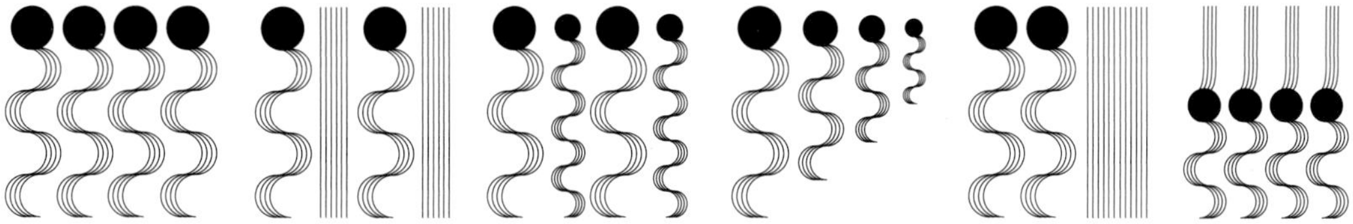

TOOL DIAMETER CHOICES

☐ ☐ ☐

WRAPPING PATTERN/DIRECTION

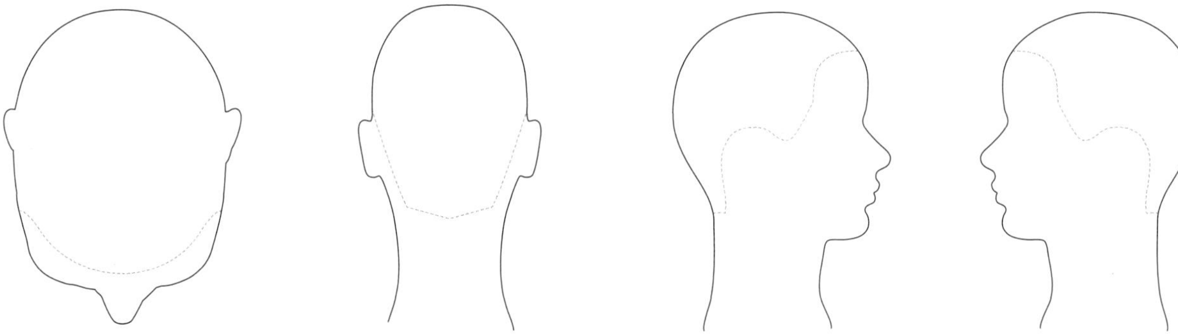

TOOL/PRODUCT CHOICE

____

____

____

Instructor Signature ______________________________ Date ______________

PERFORMANCE GUIDE
BRICKLAY PERM PATTERN OVERLAP

View the video, complete the Design Decisions chart, then perform this workshop. Complete the self-check as you progress through the workshop.

20 mins
Suggested Salon Speed

PREPARATION	✔
>> Assemble tools and products >> Set up workstation >> Shampoo hair	☐

WRAP – FRONT

1. Begin wrapping at front hairline:

>> Measure and part 1x rectangle base at center-front hairline
>> Diameter of rod
>> Project 90°
>> Single end-paper technique
>> Wrap away from face
>> Overlap technique
>> Half-off base control
>> Position pick temporarily toward face

☐

2. Measure and part diagonal bases in second row:

>> Part behind center of first perm rod
>> Measure base size using perm rod
>> Project 90°
>> Wrap and secure rod 1x half-off base
>> Repeat base control on opposite side of center part to establish one-two method

☐

3. Use the one-two method:

>> Begin next row at center again
>> Diagonal partings and 1x base size
>> Complete row
>> Begin next row with part at center again
>> Position stabilizer or picks in direction of wrap

☐

4. Adjust angle of diagonal partings as they extend to sides:

>> Work outward from center to hairline on either side for symmetry

☐

WRAP – TOP/SIDES

5. **Work toward back:**
   - >> Same wrapping technique
   - >> Adjust angle of partings and length of rod to accommodate hairline

WRAP – CROWN

6. **Transition through crown:**
   - >> Taper rows that do not extend to hairline
   - >> Same overlap technique, one-two method in these transitional rows

   Note: These rows require fewer rods than rows before and after.

7. **Decrease angle of diagonal-forward partings as you work towards nape:**
   - >> Adjust rod size to accommodate each parting
   - >> Continue working from center to hairline

WRAP – NAPE

8. **Work toward nape:**
   - >> Transitional rows as needed to work over curve of head
   - >> End with horizontal bases
   - >> Check position and base control throughout
   - >> Secure rods in direction of wrap

PROCESS/NEUTRALIZE

9. **Process and neutralize according to manufacturer's instructions.**

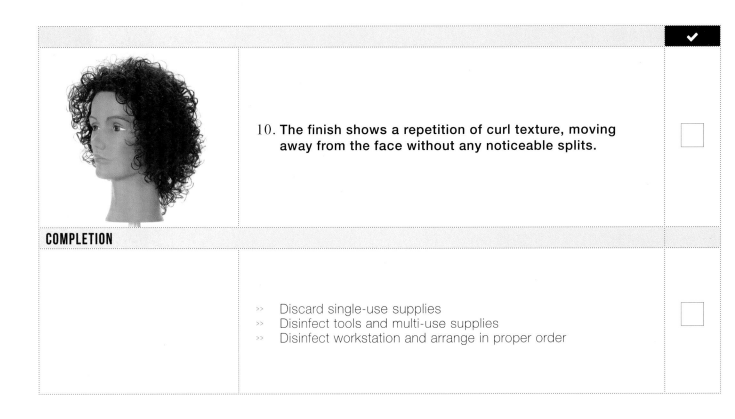

10. The finish shows a repetition of curl texture, moving away from the face without any noticeable splits.

☐

COMPLETION

>> Discard single-use supplies
>> Disinfect tools and multi-use supplies
>> Disinfect workstation and arrange in proper order

☐

20 mins
Suggested Salon Speed

My Speed
———
———
———

INSTRUCTIONS:

Record your time in comparison with the suggested salon speed. Then, list here how you could improve your performance.

_____
_____
_____
_____
_____

VARIATION — CONTOUR WRAP

A variation of the bricklay overlap wrap is available online. In this variation, larger-diameter tools are used to create soft, natural-looking texture and the fringe area is directed diagonally toward the face from a side part.

BRICKLAY PERM PATTERN
SPIRAL

EXPLORE

What client concern might lead you to consider using the spiral technique?

INSPIRE

Beautiful spiral curls, no splits and minimal visual length reduction will appeal to many clients with longer lengths who desire a natural look.

ACHIEVE

Following this *Bricklay Perm Pattern – Spiral Workshop*, you'll be able to:

» Identify the perm procedures related to the bricklay pattern – spiral

» Alternate rod diameter and wrapping direction to create a natural result

» Create an alternation of spiral curls, with no visible splits

The finished perm design shows an alternation of elongated texture on a solid form with minimal visual length reduction.

The nape is wrapped horizontally in a bricklay pattern. The spiral wrapping technique is used through the remainder of the head. Rod diameter and wrapping directions are alternated using vertical partings within horizontal sections. Note that the front is sectioned from the back, vertically from ear to ear. The front is also sectioned with a center part.

PERM PROCEDURES

1. DISTRIBUTE   N/A

2. SECTION

3. WRAP

4. PROCESS

5. NEUTRALIZE

BRICKLAY PERM PATTERN SPIRAL

Draw or fill in the boxes with the appropriate answers.

DESIGN DECISIONS

EXISTING TEXTURE

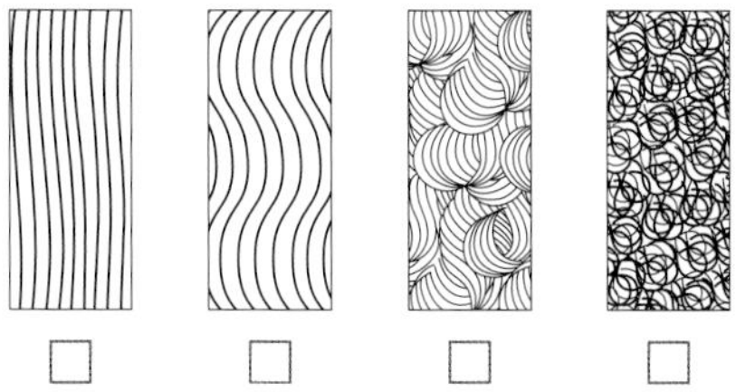

☐ ☐ ☐ ☐

DESIRED TEXTURE

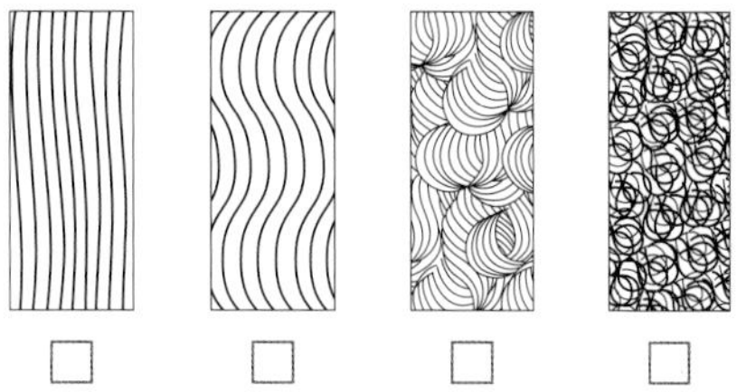

☐ ☐ ☐ ☐

TEXTURE PLACEMENT

STRAND

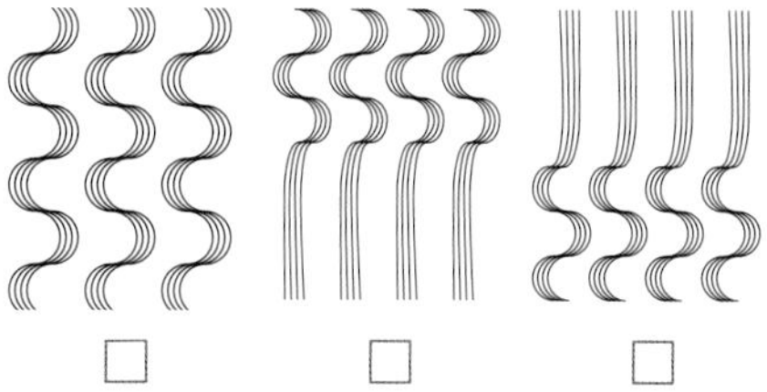

☐ ☐ ☐

DESIGN PRINCIPLES

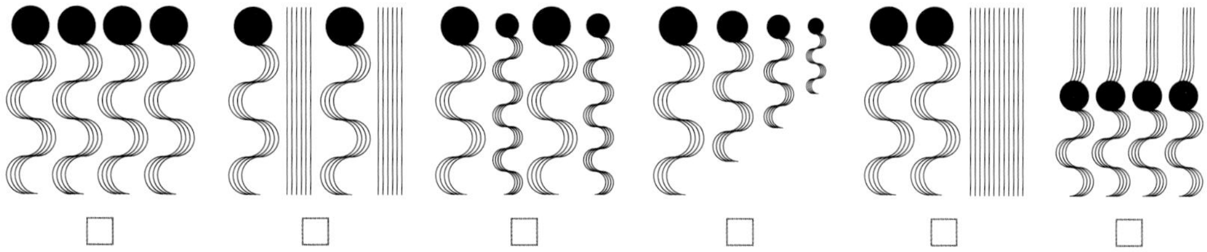

☐ ☐ ☐ ☐ ☐ ☐

TOOL DIAMETER CHOICES

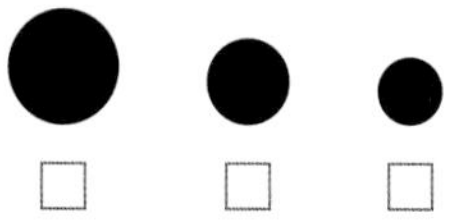

☐ ☐ ☐

WRAPPING PATTERN/DIRECTION

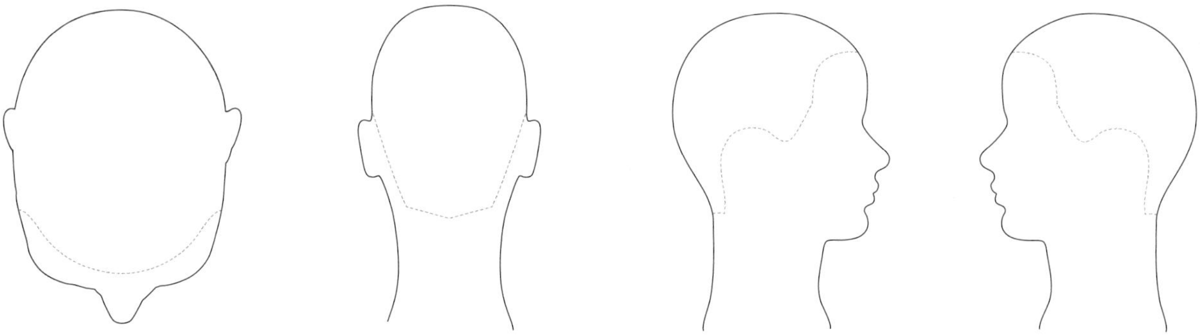

TOOL/PRODUCT CHOICE

_____

_____

_____

Instructor Signature _____ Date _____

PERFORMANCE GUIDE

BRICKLAY PERM PATTERN SPIRAL

View the video, complete the Design Decisions chart, then perform
this workshop. Complete the self-check as you progress through
the workshop.

3.5 mins
Suggested
Salon Speed

PREPARATION		✔
	>> Assemble tools and products >> Set up workstation >> Shampoo hair	☐

WRAP – NAPE

	1. **Section nape horizontally and wrap with overlap technique:** >> 1x horizontal bases >> Project 90° >> Single-end paper technique >> Half-off base control >> Short pick or stabilizers	☐

WRAP – ABOVE NAPE

	2. **Begin wrapping with spiral technique above nape:** >> Measure first horizontal row above nape with larger rod diameter >> Part vertically to create 1.5-2x base starting at right side >> Elongated bookend paper technique >> 90° projection >> Wrap toward left and position rod parallel to base >> Ends-to-base spiral wrapping technique >> Fasten rod from top to bottom >> Work toward left side using same technique	☐

3. **Measure and wrap next horizontal row:**

>> Use smaller-diameter rod
>> Begin on left side
>> Wrap towards right side with same technique

4. **Alternate rod diameters and wrapping directions with each row.**

   Note: Rods will rest in slightly different positions as you work over the curve of the head.

WRAP – SIDES

5. **Measure and wrap sides:**

>> Horizontal partings
>> Alternating rod diameter
>> Alternating directions

6. **Wrap right side:**

>> Start with larger-diameter rods
>> Horizontal parting
>> 1.5-2x base size
>> Start at ear, work toward front hairline
>> Same technique, wrap toward face

7. **Work to top of section:**
   >> Continue alternating rod diameters and wrapping directions
   >> Work up to center part
   >> Position pick or stabilizers to secure top row

8. **Repeat on opposite side:**
   >> Start with larger diameter at hairline
   >> Wrap first row toward face, beginning at ear

9. **Work to top of side:**
   >> Maintain 90° and consistent spiral wrapping technique

PROCESS/NEUTRALIZE

10. **Process and neutralize:**
   >> Position stabilizers or picks to secure top row
   >> Process and neutralize according to manufacturer's instructions

11. The spiral wrapping technique creates beautiful elongated curls on this solid form with minimal visual length reduction.

COMPLETION

>> Discard single-use supplies
>> Disinfect tools and multi-use supplies
>> Disinfect workstation and arrange in proper order

35 mins
Suggested Salon Speed

My Speed
_____
_____
_____

INSTRUCTIONS:

Record your time in comparison with the suggested salon speed. Then, list here how you could improve your performance.

_____

_____

_____

_____

_____

VARIATION – BRICKLAY SPIRAL

A variation of the bricklay spiral wrap is available online. Performed on a solid form with long layers near the face, this variation utilizes soft perm rods instead of conventional perm rods.

ZONAL PERM PATTERN

EXPLORE

Have you performed a haircut that would've benefitted from the addition of curl texture in a specific area?

INSPIRE

In the salon, customizing zonal perm patterns for shorter hairstyles will save you time and effort and set you apart as a designer.

ACHIEVE

Following this *Zonal Perm Pattern Workshop*, you'll be able to:

>> Identify the perm procedures related to the zonal perm pattern

>> Identify the appropriate-length rods to use to adapt to the specific areas of the head being permed

>> Add permed texture to the interior of a uniform/graduated combination form, using rectangular sections from a diagonal side part and a modified bricklay pattern

>> Create a uniform curl pattern in the interior, using 1x, half-off base control with woven bases to transition to unpermed exterior lengths

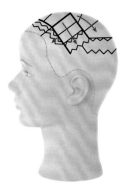

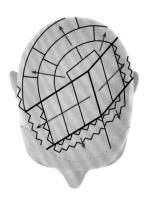

The finished perm design shows a blended curl texture on uniform and graduated layered lengths.

The front interior is wrapped from a side part to blend with the fringe, which is left natural. The rectangle on the heavier side moves toward the face. The rectangle on the lighter side moves away from the face. A modified bricklay pattern is wrapped in the remainder of the interior. Bases at the perimeter of the interior are woven.

PERM PROCEDURES

1. DISTRIBUTE

2. SECTION

3. WRAP

4. PROCESS

5. NEUTRALIZE

DESIGN DECISIONS CHART

ZONAL PERM PATTERN

Draw or fill in the boxes with the appropriate answers.

DESIGN DECISIONS

EXISTING TEXTURE

☐ ☐ ☐ ☐

DESIRED TEXTURE

☐ ☐ ☐ ☐

TEXTURE PLACEMENT

STRAND

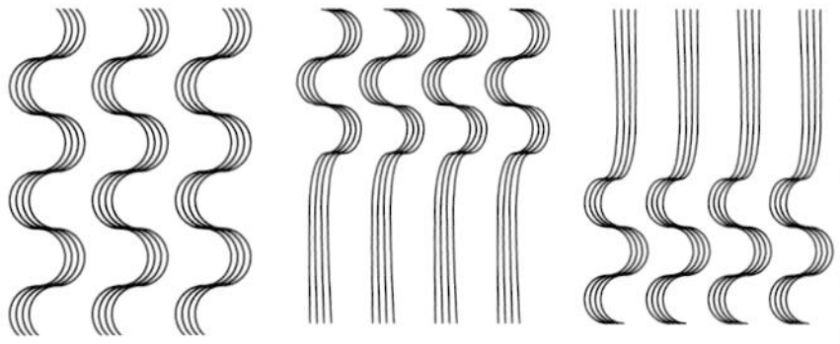

☐ ☐ ☐

DESIGN PRINCIPLES

☐ ☐ ☐ ☐ ☐ ☐

TOOL DIAMETER CHOICES

☐ ☐ ☐

WRAPPING PATTERN/DIRECTION

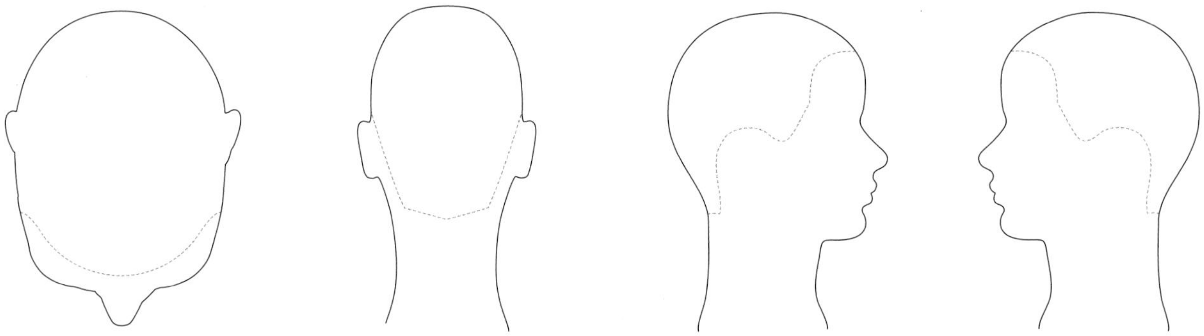

TOOL/PRODUCT CHOICE

_____

_____

_____

Instructor Signature _____ **Date** _____

ZONAL PERM PATTERN

View the video, complete the Design Decisions chart, then perform this workshop. Complete the self-check as you progress through the workshop.

1.5 mins
Suggested
Salon Speed

PREPARATION	✔

>> Assemble tools and products
>> Set up workstation
>> Shampoo hair

☐

SECTION – INTERIOR

1. Section rectangle on heavier side of interior:
>> Establish diagonal part over left eye
>> Use length of perm rod to measure width of rectangle on heavier side
>> Rectangle moves toward face
>> Incorporate some of longer fringe lengths

☐

2. Section rectangle on lighter side:
>> Same rod length
>> Rectangle moves away from face
>> Hair lengths determine remaining interior zone

☐

WRAP – INTERIOR

3. On the heavier side, part 1x base size:
>> Parallel to diagonal part
>> Bookend technique
>> Overlap technique
>> Position rod half-off base
>> Use same technique for subsequent rods in rectangle; secure as needed

☐

4. The weaving technique is used at the perimeter of the interior zone. A small section is woven off the top and secured out of the way before bottom of parting is woven.

5. **Use large-diameter perm rod to wrap last parting:**

   >> After weaving and isolating top of section, weave and wrap bottom of parting
   >> 90° projection
   >> Wrap with overlap technique

6. **Use same technique to wrap rectangle on lighter side:**

   >> Weave top and bottom of last base

   Note: Shorter lengths on this side do not require a larger-diameter rod.

7. **Wrap lengths in front of rectangle section:**

   >> Weave top and bottom of parting adjacent to section
   >> Adapt tool diameter to length of hair
   >> Overlap technique

8. **Wrap lengths behind rectangles through crown:**

   >> Release 1x parting directly behind diagonal side part
   >> Project 90°
   >> Wrap with overlap technique
   >> Position rod half-off base
   >> Continue, using bricklay pattern to avoid splits

9. **Work toward exterior:**

  >> As lengths get shorter, determine last base partings of perimeter of interior zone
  >> Weave both top and bottom
  >> Wrap with overlap technique

10. **Process and neutralize according to manufacturer's instructions.**

11. **The finish shows activated curl texture on the longer interior lengths. Note that the zonal application can also be used to create textural support for smoother finishes.**

COMPLETION

  >> Discard single-use supplies
  >> Disinfect tools and multi-use supplies
  >> Disinfect workstation and arrange in proper order

15 mins
Suggested Salon Speed

My Speed
_____
_____
_____

INSTRUCTIONS:

Record your time in comparison with the suggested salon speed. Then, list here how you could improve your performance.

_____
_____
_____
_____
_____

111C.12 //
RELAXER THEORY

EXPLORE //

Do you know someone with textured hair who is straightening it on a daily basis? There are many options today that would give them the straighter texture they desire–permanently.

INSPIRE //

Salon professionals who are skilled at performing basic relaxer services, giving their clients the looser, straighter, more relaxed styles they want, are in big demand.

ACHIEVE //

Following this lesson on *Relaxer Theory,* you'll be able to:

>> State the early breakthroughs that influenced relaxer services as we know them today

>> Name the basic relaxer services offered in salons

>> Explain the two phases involved when performing a relaxer service

FOCUS //

RELAXER THEORY

History of Relaxing

Phases of Relaxing

111ᶜ.12 | RELAXER THEORY

Look around and you'll see a variety of beautiful, natural textures in hair, from loose waves to tight curls or coils. The beauty of embracing your natural texture is that you still have the option to reduce or relax the curl pattern to achieve different looks or try new styling trends. **Relaxing refers to the loosening or reducing of the hair's existing texture as when straightening curly or tightly curled hair.**

Clients often request a relaxer service:

>> To loosen the existing texture into a gentler curl or wave

>> To straighten the hair to release as much of the texture as possible while maintaining the hair's integrity

>> To relax the hair then reintroduce some texture, known as "reforming" the hair

The maximum degree of relaxation results in straight hair; which means a small amount of texture is left in the hair. **It is not recommended that more than 85% of the natural texture is removed, as it can damage most types of hair.**

Relaxing, like perming, is a specialized service that is often performed in conjunction with other salon services, like hair sculpture, and can help you increase your income and build a loyal clientele. Although relaxer products continue to improve, making them easier and safer to use, you will see that it takes more than applying the products correctly to perform a successful relaxer service.

HISTORY OF RELAXING

The attempt to permanently relax or straighten the hair through the use of chemicals goes as far back as the early 20th century.

The first chemical relaxers were:

>> An unstable formula, and produced unpredictable results; usually so strong it caused hair loss and severe scalp burns

>> Made of potash (wood ashes), lye, white potatoes and lard. Mixed together, these produced a harsh mixture strong enough to chemically straighten tightly curled hair.

>> A caustic chemical in its purest form which used lye as the active ingredient and had a pH of 14. Lye has the ability to eat away or erode the cuticle layer of the hair, making it very limp and straight

>> A later variation that included eggs and was called "Congolene" or "Conk" for short: the resulting "Conk" style which was worn predominantly by African American male musicians and entertainers trying to fit in with mainstream audiences

In the early 1900s, a temporary method of hair relaxing called hair pressing, was conceived by Sarah Breedlove (1867-1919), who was better known as Madam C. J. Walker.

Early hair pressing involved:

>> Petroleum jelly applied to hair after it had been washed and dried

>> A metal comb, heated over a small gas burner, which was then pressed against and pulled through the hair using tension, temporarily straightening it

BLACK HERITAGE
32 USA
Madam C. J. Walker
1998

The first straightener product for human hair was successfully marketed as G. A. Morgan Hair Refining Cream.

>> Garrett A. Morgan was an inventor who greatly impacted society with his "smoke hood," a safety hood smoke protection device that saved many lives, and with his three-position automatic traffic signal.

>> Morgan is credited with developing the first human hair straightener.

   ▨ In early 1900s, in his efforts to develop a useful polish to reduce friction in sewing machine needles, he discovered that the liquid straightened the animal-hair fibers in a piece of cloth he had wiped his hands on. After additional experimentation, he tested the formula on his own hair—which he was able to straighten.

By the late 1950s, several commercially produced chemical relaxers were available. Even though they remained highly caustic with the potential to cause damage to hair and scalp, the new formulas were more consistent, and predictable results were possible.

BASIC RELAXER SERVICES

There are four basic relaxer services: curl diffusion, virgin relaxer, retouch relaxer and zonal relaxer. These four services comprise the relaxer services you will perform most frequently in the salon. Although trends and salons, as well as product manufacturers will use different descriptive names and varied techniques, the principles and techniques from these core relaxer services will serve as the foundation.

A **curl diffusion** service, also known as a chemical blow-out, is a technique used to loosen or relax tightly curled hair patterns by approximately 50% of their natural shape.

A **virgin relaxer** service is a technique used on natural, untreated or "virgin" hair to straighten the hair up to 85%.

A **retouch relaxer** service is performed on the new growth only to match the previously relaxed hair.

A **zonal relaxer** service is performed only in selected areas of the head. A zonal relaxer is usually performed when the client's nape area and sides are closely tapered or when the perimeter hairline is frizzy.

PHASES OF RELAXING

As in perming, relaxing the hair involves both chemical and physical steps, which are equally important. In relaxing, the chemical and physical phases are not as clear-cut as in perming. This is because the relaxer chemical is applied early in the procedure, then the physical steps of smoothing the hair and testing are performed. After the relaxer chemical is rinsed, the neutralizer is applied and rinsed. The following information will give you a brief overview of the steps involved in the chemical and physical phases of a relaxer service.

For more detailed information refer to the lesson on *Relaxer Products and Essentials* as well as *Relaxer Skills.*

CHEMICAL PHASE

The relaxer service begins with the chemical phase, which involves:

>> Sectioning the hair

>> Applying the relaxer product

Section

>> Performed for better organization and control of the application of the relaxer product

After sectioning, a base cream is applied to protect the skin around the hairline and ears. See the *Relaxer Skills* lesson for more information on basing.

Apply

After sectioning the hair, you will apply the chemical relaxer product, usually containing either sodium hydroxide or ammonium thioglycolate. Sodium hydroxide, is the stronger of the two most commonly used chemical relaxers.

You will generally choose:

Sodium hydroxide
>> For tightly curled or resistant hair

>> May be more irritating; requires base cream applied to the entire scalp, hairline and ears

Ammonium thioglycolate
>> Often called "thio"

>> For wavy to curly hair

>> Not as strong or harsh as sodium hydroxide relaxers

>> Does not require base cream to be applied to the scalp

The relaxer chemical is applied with an application brush. Applying the proper strength relaxer product based on the client's hair type is critical to the success of the relaxer service.

Refer to the lesson on *Relaxer Skills* for more detailed information on relaxer procedures.

PHYSICAL PHASE

The success or failure of a chemical relaxer service is strongly influenced by the physical phase of the service. The second phase of a relaxer service, the physical phase, involves:

>> Smoothing or combing the hair

>> Timing and testing

>> Rinsing and blotting

>> Neutralizing

Smooth or Comb

The physical phase begins with smoothing or combing the hair while the chemical relaxer product is on it. Smoothing facilitates relaxation and reforming of bonds to new straighter position.

Time and Test

Knowing how long to smooth the relaxer product through the hair is critical to achieving the desired texture result. Rinsing too soon, or leaving the relaxer on too long will both lead to a dissatisfied client.

Two primary ways to know when to stop smoothing and rinse the relaxer from the hair are:

1. Timing according to manufacturer's directions and/or standard salon guidelines

2. Performing relaxation tests, also know as comb tests, to determine whether hair is relaxed to the desired degree or whether more smoothing is required

Always follow manufacturer's instructions for timing and testing. See the *Relaxer Skills* lesson for specific information on timing and testing.

Rinse and Blot

The hair is rinsed for a long time to remove any chemical residue and to stop the chemical action. Any relaxer product left behind can severely damage the hair and scalp.

Blotting removes excess water so that the neutralizing product or neutralizing shampoo work more effectively.

Neutralize

The last step of the physical phase of a relaxer service is neutralizing. For relaxers with a sodium hydroxide-based product, a neutralizing shampoo is used; with ammonium thioglycolate-based products, a neutralizing solution is used. Neutralizing forms the hair into its new texture pattern. Always follow manufacturer's instructions when neutralizing the hair.

You'll learn more about types of relaxers, applying/smoothing techniques and neutralizing in upcoming lessons.

SALON**CONNECTION**

Clients who have embraced their natural texture or temporarily straightened their hair, may now want to relax or straighten their hair permanently. Yet, they may have reservations based on prior experiences. As you learn more about what can be achieved with the relaxers and straighteners on the market today, you can help these clients feel comfortable with the new possibilities and benefits of relaxer services.

Your specialized skills in providing chemical relaxer services will allow you to transform your clients' appearance, allowing them to enjoy the looser, straighter, more relaxed styles they want.

LESSONS LEARNED

Relaxing refers to the loosening or reducing of the hair's existing texture as when straightening curly or tightly curled hair.

Several early breakthroughs that influenced relaxer services include:

>> The attempt to permanently relax or straighten the hair goes as far back as the early 20th century.

>> First relaxers were made of potash (wood ashes), lye, white potatoes and lard, producing a harsh mixture strong enough to chemically straighten tightly curled hair.

>> In the early 1900s a temporary method of hair relaxing called hair pressing, was conceived by Sarah Breedlove (1867-1919), who was better known as Madam C. J. Walker.

>> Garrett A. Morgan is credited with developing the first straightener product for human hair.

There are four basic relaxer services: curl diffusion, virgin relaxer, retouch relaxer and zonal relaxer.

There are two phases involved in performing a relaxer: the chemical phase and physical phase.

>> Chemical phase – Involves sectioning the hair and applying the relaxer product

>> Physical phase – Involves smoothing or combing the hair, testing for relaxation and neutralizing

111^c.13
RELAXER PRODUCTS & ESSENTIALS

EXPLORE //

What are the proper tools and products that will allow you to perform relaxer services that result in optimum shine, manageability and styling ease?

INSPIRE // As you take your client from curly to straight hair, your choice of products and tools is vital to maintaining the integrity of the hair.

ACHIEVE // Following this lesson on *Relaxer Products and Essentials,* you'll be able to:

>> Explain the types of relaxer products and their usage

>> Describe the functions of the main tools used for relaxing

>> Provide examples of products, supplies and equipment used to perform a relaxer service

FOCUS // **RELAXER PRODUCTS AND ESSENTIALS**

Relaxer Products

Relaxer Essentials

RELAXER PRODUCTS AND ESSENTIALS

To perform professional relaxer services, you need a selection of products, tools, supplies and equipment.

RELAXER PRODUCTS

Relaxers can provide maximum relaxing action as well as optimum conditioning. When applied and handled correctly they cause minimal or no scalp irritation or hair breakage and leave the hair shiny and healthy in its newly relaxed texture state.

Although there are many relaxer products used in the professional salon, they fall into two major categories:

» Sodium hydroxide
- Stronger of the two chemicals
- More relaxing power than ammonium thioglycolate
- More caustic and harsher to clients' hair, scalp and skin
  » Used on:
    - Curly
    - Tightly curled
    - Resistant hair

» Ammonium thioglycolate
  » Used on:
    - Wavy
    - Curly
    - Nonresistant hair

Understanding each type of relaxer product will enable you to choose the most appropriate product for each individual client.

TYPES OF RELAXER PRODUCTS

ALERT!

Do not apply sodium hydroxide relaxer to extremely porous hair that has been colored with permanent hair color or lightened hair (decolorized, bleached). Also, do not apply sodium hydroxide to hair that has been permed or relaxed previously with ammonium thioglycolate. Multiple services performed over the hair reduce the number of bonds in the hair, which can result in severe breakage.

Sodium Hydroxide

Sodium hydroxide relaxers:

>> Formulated with 2% to 3% sodium hydroxide in a heavy cream base

>> Are a strong alkaline product

>> Have an alkaline pH of 11.5-14

>> Designed to straighten tightly curled hair

>> Also known as:
- Sodium relaxers
- Lye relaxers

>> Prior to the 1960s they were known as base relaxers because they required a base cream applied prior to the relaxer to protect the scalp

>> Following the 1960s, no-base sodium relaxers have become the choice of salon professionals because they are gentler to the hair and scalp

>> No-base sodium relaxers:

- Contain oil and conditioning agents to protect the hair and scalp from irritation

- Still contain caustic chemical, which requires skill and product knowledge

- Base cream is still needed for clients with a sensitive scalp

---

It is important to remember that the chemical action of a sodium hydroxide relaxer is irreversible. Follow manufacturer's directions for safe and accurate results.

No-lye relaxers:

>> Contain a derivative of sodium hydroxide

>> They contain one of the following active ingredients:
- Calcium
- Potassium
- Guanidine
- Lithium hydroxide or bisulfate

>> Recommended for less resistant hair and require frequent follow-up conditioning treatments

---

Ammonium Thioglycolate

Ammonium thioglycolate (thio) relaxer:

>> Formulated with 4% to 6% thioglycolic acid or its derivatives with 1% ammonium hydroxide

>> Cream base is also usually added

>> pH of 8.5-9.5

>> Chemical reducing agent that causes hair to soften and swell

>> Affects the hydrogen and disulfide bonds during processing:

- Disulfide bonds break between the two sulfur atoms in the cysteine amino acids

- Neutralizing process causes the split cysteine amino acids to rejoin

>> Relaxer strengths are categorized as:

- Mild (delicate) – Used on healthy, color-treated hair, fine-textured or porous hair

- Regular (normal) – Used on curly to medium-textured hair

- Super (resistant) – Used on tightly curled, coarse-textured or resistant hair

---

Ammonium Thioglycolate Relaxers: 8.5-9.5   *Sodium Hydroxide Relaxers: 11.5-14.0*

SALONCONNECTION
Relaxing and Coloring

Hair color services requiring hydrogen peroxide should not be performed on the same day as the relaxer service and should generally wait 10 days. However, hair color services using a nonoxidative color product (temporary or semi-permanent) can be performed the same day. Relaxer services should never be combined with color services that require lightener (bleach).

Sodium, no-lye and thio relaxer formulas consist of three principle ingredients that control the relaxer's effectiveness and efficiency:

>> Active alkaline agent (sodium, potassium, lithium or guanidine hydroxide)

>> Oil (surfactants or surface-acting agents that protect the hair and scalp)

>> Water

Remember that the chemical formulation of the chemical relaxer requires a quick application, processing and removal to prevent damage.

ALERT!

Sodium hydroxide and thioglycolate are NOT compatible. A sodium hydroxide relaxer should never be performed on hair that has been relaxed with a thioglycolate relaxer, or vice versa.

NEUTRALIZER

Prior to neutralizing, the relaxer product must be rinsed thoroughly from the hair to stop the chemical action and remove any chemical residues. When the hair is free of chemicals and excess moisture (blotted), proceed with the neutralizing shampoo procedure. **It is important to use an acid-balanced neutralizing shampoo or stabilizer to reharden (lock) the hair into its new, straighter shape.**

Neutralizer:
>> Shampoo or lotion

>> Reduces swelling caused by alkaline formulas

>> Causes oxidation, which restores broken down disulfide bonds

>> Results in hair being held in new straight configuration

>> pH 2.5-7.0

Neutralize sodium hydroxide-based relaxers with a neutralizing shampoo.

Neutralize ammonium thioglycolate with a neutralizing solution.

Follow manufacturer's directions regarding how many times to shampoo the hair and how long the neutralizing product should be left on the hair.

PRODUCT OVERVIEW

The following chart summarizes the different types of chemical relaxer products along with the advantages and disadvantages of each. This chart can be used as a guide when choosing the proper relaxer for any type of hair. Remember to also consider the strength of the relaxer.

TYPE AND DESCRIPTION (LISTED BY MAIN INGREDIENT)	ADVANTAGE	DISADVANTAGE
Sodium Hydroxide Category: Lye, Base, No Base pH: 11.5 - 14	Faster processing time; better for resistant hair and/or coarse hair	Irritates the scalp; may cause severe damage; strict time constraints; base application required and/or recommended
Calcium or Potassium Hydroxide Category: No Lye	Better for less-resistant hair; less irritating to scalp	May be more drying; slower processing time; requires frequent conditioning treatments
Guanidine Hydroxide Category: No Lye, Mix (contains calcium hydroxide and guanidine carbonate)	Better for less-resistant hair; less irritating to scalp	Processes slowly; not recommended for tightly curled hair
Lithium Hydroxide Category: No Lye, No Mix	Better for less-resistant hair; less irritating to scalp	Processes slowly; not recommended for tightly curled hair
Ammonium Bisulfate Category: No Lye, No Mix	Better for less-resistant hair	Requires the addition of heat; not recommended for tightly curled hair
Ammonium Thioglycolate pH: 8.5 - 9.5	Better for less-resistant hair; more control due to processing time; better for fragile, fine or tinted hair	Not recommended for tightly curled hair

DISCOVER**MORE**

Take the time to research new products, developments and education in the relaxer market. Relaxer services are evolving with advancements in formulations and products to protect the hair and keep it in the best possible condition. These advancements give you more options to choose from so you can provide exceptional relaxer services.

Keep in mind, employers are required to make Safety Data Sheets (SDS) for all products available for your reference and use in the salon.

Relaxer products are produced by many different manufacturers, are disposable and must be frequently replaced.

PRODUCTS	FUNCTION
Shampoo	Cleanses/removes dirt and oils from scalp and hair
Base Cream	Protects scalp, hairline and ears from chemicals; petroleum-based product
Protective Cream	Protects parts of hairstrand not being processed during a retouch service
Chemical Relaxer Product	Relaxes hair texture
Neutralizer or Neutralizing Shampoo	Rehardens, fixes and restores bonds to make new shape of hair permanent; contains oxidizing agent
Protein/Moisturizing Conditioner/Sealer	Restores protein and/or moisture balance lost during processing
Styling Lotion	Provides extra control and lasting quality of design
Styling Products	Provide extra flexibility and holding qualities of design

RELAXER ESSENTIALS

The following charts will help you become familiar with the various tools, supplies and equipment you will use for relaxer services in the salon.

RELAXER TOOLS

TOOLS	FUNCTION
Applicator Brush	Applies relaxer and neutralizer to hair with less product waste, greater control and efficiency
Plastic Bowl	Holds the relaxer product during application
Tail Comb (Non-Metal)	Parts out sections of hair; used for smoothing during processing
Shampoo Comb	Distributes neutralizer through the hair, eliminating tangles and minimizing damage to swollen hair using smooth, wide teeth of the comb

RELAXER SUPPLIES

SUPPLIES	FUNCTION
Protective Shampoo Cape	Protects client from chemicals; large, loose protective covering fastened at the neck area
Cloth Towels	Absorb and remove water, relaxer product and neutralizer when blotting
Neutralizing Bib/Neutralizing Cape	Catches excess chemicals as they run off the scalp; protects client
Protective Apron/Smock for Stylist	Protect stylist's clothing from relaxer product
Spatula	Removes relaxer and/or other products from containers for application, keeping supply of original product uncontaminated
Protective Gloves	Protect designer's hands from chemicals during processing
Plastic Sectioning Clips	Hold hair in place for easier application of relaxer products
Chemical Service Record	Documents client's personal and relaxer information

RELAXER EQUIPMENT

EQUIPMENT	FUNCTION
Heat Equipment: Plastic Cap, Infrared Lamps, Hood Dryer	Provide and capture heat when conditioning following relaxer service; help restore hair's structural integrity
Timer	Alerts stylist to check for appropriate amount of time allowed for relaxer to be on hair and scalp; also for monitoring neutralizing times as recommended by manufacturer
Shampoo Bowl	Allows client's hair to be rinsed and shampooed; needed for rinsing relaxer chemicals and neutralizer from hair
Styling Chair	Adjusts for designer's working needs and comfortable seating for client

Understanding the different relaxer product and tool choices available allows you to make your selection based on the desired end result and your client's hair type—while maintaining the integrity of the hair.

LESSONS LEARNED

The two main relaxer products and their usage include:
>> Sodium hydroxide:
  ▓ Strong alkaline product

  ▓ pH of 11.5-14

  ▓ Designed to straighten tightly curled hair

>> Ammonium thioglycolate:
  ▓ pH of 8.5-9.5

  ▓ Chemical reducing agent that causes hair to soften and swell

  ▓ Affect the hydrogen and disulfide bonds during thio processing

Other products used in a relaxer service include base cream, protective cream, and neutralizing shampoo or lotion.

The tools used to perform relaxer services include the applicator brush, a non-metal tail comb and a shampoo comb.

Relaxer essentials include the supplies and equipment that are needed to perform a relaxer service.

>> Supplies include the cape, cloth towels, protective gloves and plastic sectioning clips

>> Equipment includes permanent fixtures such as the hydraulic chair, timer and shampoo bowl

111ᶜ.14 //
RELAXER SKILLS

EXPLORE //

Being proficient in the skills needed to perform a relaxer service requires practice, practice and more practice! What kind of results can you expect if you are "out of practice"?

INSPIRE //

Following procedures while performing relaxer services will help you achieve consistent and predictable relaxer results for your steady and growing clientele.

ACHIEVE //

Following this lesson on *Relaxer Skills*, you'll be able to:

>> Explain how the hair is analyzed prior to the relaxer service

>> Identify and explain the five procedural steps during the relaxer service

FOCUS //

RELAXER SKILLS

Pre-Relaxer Analysis

Relaxer Procedures

Careful analysis of your client's hair and your ability to apply relaxer skills at the required speed will allow you to successfully relax your client's hair while maintaining its integrity. In *Relaxer Skills*, you'll focus on pre-relaxer analysis and the procedural steps used to carry out your relaxer plans.

111ᶜ.14 | RELAXER SKILLS

Conducting several preliminary tests before a chemical service will help you gain the most accurate assessment possible of your client's hair to ensure optimal results. As you perform these tests, carefully analyze the condition of the hair and scalp. If you see signs of breakage in the hair or abrasions on the scalp, postpone the service until the condition improves.

PRE-RELAXER ANALYSIS

Before beginning a relaxer service, properly assess the condition of your client's hair. The porosity, elasticity, texture, density, type of curl pattern and overall condition of the hair will help you determine:

>> The appropriate type of relaxer service

>> Type and strength of relaxer product

>> Amount and time of combing or smoothing required

POROSITY

Porosity refers to the ability of the hair to absorb moisture, liquids or chemicals. Porosity is also one of the determining factors in selecting the appropriate chemical relaxer strength and processing time.

Some key guidelines that will help you select the appropriate relaxer product are:

Extreme Porosity

Resistant Porosity

>> The more porous the hair, the faster the hair will accept the product.

>> With porous hair, choose a product labeled as mild.

>> When the hair is more resistant, you will need to select a stronger product, sometimes labeled as super strength.

POROSITY TEST

The following test, also known as a finger test, will help you determine hair porosity.

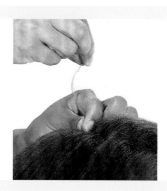

>> Run your thumb and finger along a strand of hair against the direction of growth (ends to base). If the hair feels rough it will be due to the cuticle scales being raised and open, which is an indication that the hair is more porous and therefore damaged.

>> Record results in client's record.

ELASTICITY

Elasticity is the hair's ability to stretch and return to its original shape without breaking, much like the action of a rubber band. Elasticity can range from very good to very poor.

The elasticity test is also known as the pull test. Refer to the *Perm Skills* lesson to see how to perform this test.

Hair with good elasticity	Hair with poor elasticity
Flexes back and forth as it is gently pulled	Requires milder chemicals
Can usually tolerate stronger chemicals	If not extreme, you may chemically relax the hair and offer a course of treatment following the relaxer service
	In case of extreme breakage, you may need to cut off the damaged hair before a relaxer service
	If the hair has very poor elasticity, chemicals should not be used at all

SALON**CONNECTION**

The Effects of Porosity

Stylists often ask clients how well their hair holds a curl when styled with curly or wavy texture. Hair that holds styled curls well usually has lower porosity and better elasticity than hair that loses curls quickly.

TEXTURE

Another aspect of texture relates to the actual size or diameter of an individual hairstrand. **In this aspect, texture can be categorized as fine, medium or coarse.**

Commonly one head of hair may have several different textures, such as very fine hair in the nape area and coarse hair in the crown. In this instance, choose a relaxer suited for the finer texture.

Conduct a strand test on each type of hair texture, even if this means testing in several different areas of the head.

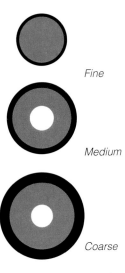

Fine

Medium

Coarse

Identifying Natural Texture Patterns

Natural texture patterns, also called curl patterns, can be identified by their visual characteristics. The four major texture patterns as determined by the shape of the hair follicle are:

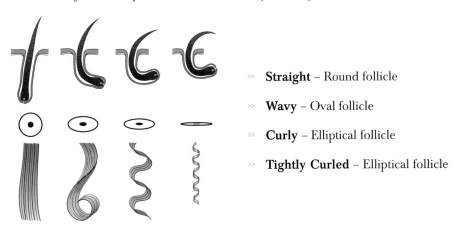

>> **Straight** – Round follicle

>> **Wavy** – Oval follicle

>> **Curly** – Elliptical follicle

>> **Tightly Curled** – Elliptical follicle

Tightly curled hair is also referred to as flat-cell hair because of its flat shape. Although certain ethnicities are often associated with particular textures, all of the texture patterns can be found in people of every ethnicity and race. It is also common for one person's head of hair to have several different texture patterns, such as both straight and wavy.

Three curl patterns that primarily relate to relaxing services are:

>> **Wavy**

>> **Curly**

>> **Tightly Curled**

STAGES OF RELAXING TIGHTLY CURLED HAIR

Relaxing tightly curled hair to the 100% relaxation level can overprocess the hair, leaving it limp and susceptible to breakage. Even without removing 100% of the hair's texture, relaxing tightly curled hair can give clients a wide range of hair design options.

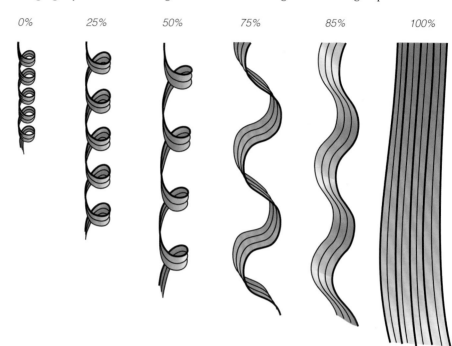

0%   25%   50%   75%   85%   100%

Tightly Curled Texture Pattern

>> 0% – Not Relaxed

Relaxing

>> 25% – Minimum Relaxing

>> 50% – Curl Diffusion

>> 75% – S-Curl Pattern

Optimum Relaxing

>> 85%

Overprocessed

>> 100%

Before beginning to create your texture design, it is important to think through the amount of texture you want to reduce. This will determine which relaxer service and therefore, which procedure you will follow.

To loosen—not straighten—curly to tightly curled hair into a freer, more moveable curl pattern, perform a service called curl diffusion, sometimes referred to as texturizing.

Curl Diffusion

To remove even more texture from curly or tightly curled hair, perform a relaxer service using either ammonium thioglycolate- or sodium hydroxide-based products.

Relaxer

DENSITY

Density refers to the number of hair follicles per square inch and can be classified as either light, medium or heavy (sometimes low, medium, high). Knowing the hair's density helps you determine the proper size partings to use during the relaxer application. For example, thick or high density will require smaller and, therefore, more partings than thin or low density.

RELAXER PROCEDURES

Knowing the procedures for producing predictable relaxer results and performing them with purpose and appropriate speed can help focus attention on what's important so that you get the desired outcome.

The chemical phase in relaxing includes sectioning the hair and applying the relaxer product. The physical phase includes smoothing or combing the hair, performing relaxation tests and neutralizing.

Regardless of the service chosen, the relaxing procedure progresses through these five steps:

CHEMICAL PHASE		PHYSICAL PHASE		

Section   *Apply*   *Comb or Smooth*   *Test*   *Neutralize*

SECTION

The first procedure step is to section the hair for organization and control during the chemical application process. Generally, you will create four or five large sections when relaxing the entire head.

For partial or zonal relaxer services:

>> Section a certain area or zone, such as the top, fringe, sides or nape

>> Section only in the areas where texture will be loosened or straightened

Base

Before applying the chemical relaxer product on the client's hair and scalp, it is important to protect the skin around the hairline and ears with a base cream (basing). Base cream is always applied to the entire scalp when using a sodium hydroxide relaxer or if a client who is receiving a thio relaxer has a history of scalp sensitivity.

Petroleum is the main ingredient in base creams. Body heat liquefies the base, providing a light, oily film that helps protect the scalp from irritation during chemical processing.

Base is applied to the entire scalp using a checkerboard technique:

» Horizontal then vertical partings are used to apply the base to the scalp.

» Base cream is applied with a dabbing motion, as rubbing might sensitize the scalp.

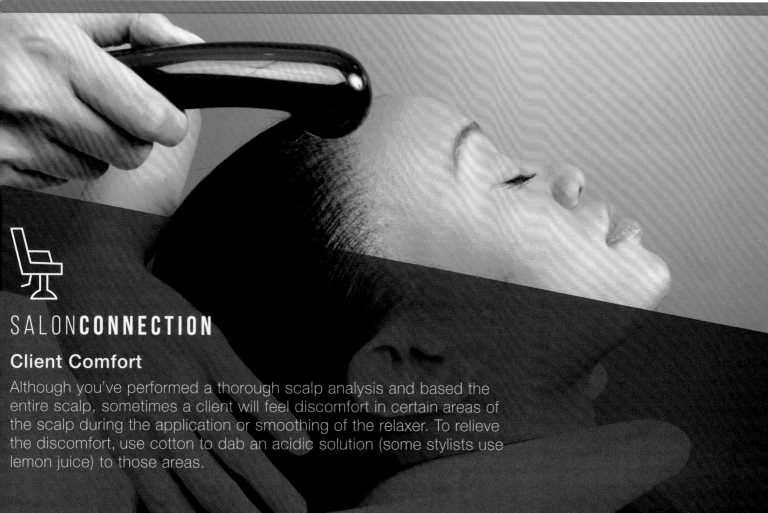

SALON**CONNECTION**

Client Comfort

Although you've performed a thorough scalp analysis and based the entire scalp, sometimes a client will feel discomfort in certain areas of the scalp during the application or smoothing of the relaxer. To relieve the discomfort, use cotton to dab an acidic solution (some stylists use lemon juice) to those areas.

APPLY

Applying accurately and efficiently in addition to working with the proper strength relaxer product based on the client's hair type is critical to the success of the relaxer service. The following points are good to know when applying relaxer:

>> The primary application method is with a brush.

>> Product is applied to one or both sides of the strand depending on the requirements of the service being performed.

>> Apply relaxer evenly, without missing any areas to prevent an uneven pattern of straight or curly hair or ridges that could be hard to control.

See additional application information specific to different relaxer services below:

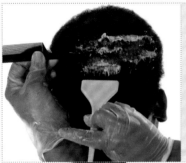

Curl Diffusion
>> Product generally applied to shorter lengths of hair

>> Tail comb used to section and control hair

>> Brush used to apply product to surface of hair

Virgin Relaxer
>> Relaxer first applied to most resistant area (usually crown or lower)

>> First applied ¼" (.6 cm) to ½" (1.25 cm) away from scalp area, up to porous ends

>> Next applied to area near scalp

Chemical relaxers have a tendency to spread toward the scalp due to body heat, so further application may not be needed.

Retouch Relaxer
>> Uses same procedures as virgin application, except product is applied only to new growth area near scalp

>> Overlapping product onto previously relaxed hair may result in breakage

>> Apply protective cream to previously treated hair

Zonal Relaxer
Relaxer is applied to selected areas of head.

Depending on the desired result:

>> Use curl diffusion application technique

>> Use virgin relaxer application technique

Several manufacturers have created chemical hair straightening and relaxer systems that do not strictly adhere to basic relaxing procedures. These may include the addition of a heat source (thermal reconditioning) or the addition of a chemical treatment. As a hair professional, you will want to be acquainted with new products and innovations. Research online various chemical hair straightening/relaxer products and systems. Note that some of these systems might be considered advanced—to be tried once you have more experience with more basic methods. Seek out training opportunities to gain competence in performing such services.

COMB OR SMOOTH

Smoothing redistributes the relaxer on the hairstrand and helps relax and reform the bonds to a new straighter position.

In typical relaxer services:

>> Smoothing means to use the spine or back of the comb to work the relaxer through the hair and achieve the desired degree of relaxation

>> Smoothing is performed from base to ends in a downward direction for virgin applications

>> For retouch applications be careful not to overlap or smooth previously relaxed hair

Remember that it is not advisable to completely straighten tightly curled hair 100%, as it will cause breakage.

In a curl diffusion service:

>> Comb (instead of smoothing) the relaxer through the hair to reduce the curl pattern only by about 50%

>> Combing with the teeth of the comb, rather than smoothing with the back of the comb, ensures that the hair is not overly relaxed beyond the 50% level

>> Be sure not to strip relaxer product off the hair while combing

Timing and Testing

The two primary ways to know when you can stop smoothing and rinse the relaxer from the hair are:

1. Timing according to manufacturer's directions and/or standard salon guidelines

2. Performing relaxation tests

TIMING GUIDE

When the chemical relaxer is applied, it softens and swells the hair, allowing penetration through the cuticle into the cortex layer where the sulfur and hydrogen bonds are altered. These bonds contribute to the hair's elasticity, strength and resilience, while helping retain its curly state.

The texture and porosity control how quickly or slowly the chemical relaxer penetrates:

>> Coarse-texture hair

    ▦ Generally less cuticle and more cortex

    ▦ Slower product absorption

    ▦ Increased processing time, especially if the hair is nonporous (highly resistant)

>> Fine-texture hair

    ▦ More cuticle and less cortex

    ▦ Relaxer product may initially take longer to penetrate to cortex, yet can quickly damage the inner layer

    ▦ Requires a sound knowledge of its structure and the effects of chemicals

The following timing charts can be used as guide for application and smoothing.

THIO RELAXERS		
STRENGTH	**CONDITION OF HAIR**	**TIMING**
Mild	Color Treated and/or Fine-Texture Hair	Up to 15 minutes
Regular	Curly to Medium-Texture Hair	Up to 20 minutes
Super	Tightly Curled to Coarse-Texture Hair	Up to 25 minutes

SODIUM HYDROXIDE RELAXERS		
STRENGTH	**CONDITION OF HAIR**	**TIMING**
Mild	Color Treated and/or Fine-Texture Hair	10 to 15 minutes
Regular	Curly to Medium-Texture Hair	Up to 20 minutes
Super	Tightly Curled to Coarse-Texture Hair	Up to 20 minutes

Keep in mind that these charts are only a guide and timing may be affected by the hair's condition, including porosity.

RELAXATION TEST

The **relaxation test, also known as the comb test,** allows you to determine when the hair is relaxed enough or whether additional smoothing is required. Always follow manufacturer's instructions for timing and testing.

For virgin and retouch relaxer services, the relaxation test includes two steps:

1. Clear away excess product from the base or near scalp area using the back or tail of the comb.

2. Press the back or tail of the comb against hair near scalp area and assess amount of indentation that occurs.

   a. If the curl pattern reverts or "beads," additional smoothing may be required.

   b. If a strong amount of indentation occurs, the hair has reached optimum relaxation and is ready to rinse and blot.

For curl diffusion services, testing depends on your visual perception to know when the desired degree of curl has been achieved. As you comb the hair, watch for how the hair "springs" back. Continue to comb the hair until you reach the desired degree of curl.

Rinsing and Blotting

The following are points to remember when rinsing and blotting the hair:

>> Because of the high alkalinity of relaxers, the hair must be rinsed for a long period of time to stop the chemical action and completely rid the hair of any chemical residues.

>> Check closely in the nape area and behind the ears, which are areas that are more difficult to rinse.

>> Any chemicals left in the hair will remain active and could cause serious skin and/or hair damage.

>> Blotting the hair to remove excess water after rinsing is also very important. Excess moisture left on the hair can adversely affect the ability of the neutralizer to work properly.

>> Blotting also gives you the opportunity to check carefully throughout the entire scalp area for any chemicals that have not been rinsed.

Be extremely gentle but thorough, as the hair is in a weakened state at this point.

NEUTRALIZE

When you are certain the hair is free of chemicals and excess moisture, proceed with the neutralizing procedure. **Use an acid-balanced neutralizing shampoo or stabilizer to reharden (lock) the hair into its new, straighter shape.** The neutralizer causes oxidation, which restores the broken disulfide bonds. Always be guided by the manufacturer's directions about how many times you must shampoo the hair and how long the neutralizing product is to be left on the hair.

For hair relaxer services that utilize a sodium hydroxide-based product, a neutralizing shampoo is used to reharden the hair into its new, straighter shape.

With an ammonium thioglycolate-based product, use a neutralizing solution, rather than a shampoo, to form the hair into its new texture pattern. Always follow manufacturer's instructions when neutralizing the hair.

Sodium hydroxide raises the pH level of the hair, while neutralizer or neutralizing shampoo lowers the pH level. Although you can choose to condition/moisturize the hair before or after the neutralizing step, doing it before allows for deeper penetration of the moisturizer or conditioner.

CREATING THE NEW RELAXED CURL PATTERN

The following steps provide a guide of how you will create new, relaxed texture patterns for your clients.

1. Identify the existing texture pattern:	Wavy, curly, tightly curled
2. Determine the desired texture pattern:	Straight, wavy, curly
3. Analyze hair competency:	Porosity, elasticity, density
4. Select the appropriate relaxer service:	Curl diffusion, virgin, retouch, zonal (or partial)
5. Choose the relaxer product and formula:	Thio or sodium; mild, regular, super
6. Perform the relaxer service.	

Understanding the procedures and practicing the skills involved in relaxer services will help you expand your expertise as well as your client base.

LESSONS LEARNED

During a pre-relaxer analysis, the following is analyzed:

>> Porosity – The ability of the hair to absorb moisture, liquids or chemicals

>> Elasticity – The hair's ability to stretch and return without breaking

>> Texture – The actual size or diameter of an individual hairstrand

>> Density – Refers to the number of hair follicles per square inch and can be classified as either light, medium and/or heavy (sometimes thin, medium, thick)

Regardless of the service chosen, the relaxer procedure progresses through these five steps: Section, Apply, Comb or Smooth, Test, and Neutralize.

>> Generally, you will create four or five large sections when relaxing the entire head.

>> Before applying the chemical relaxer product on the client's hair and scalp, it is important to protect the skin around the hairline and ears with a base cream (basing).

>> The primary method of applying relaxer products is with a brush.

>> Smoothing redistributes the relaxer on the hairstrand and helps relax and reform the bonds to a new, straighter position.

>> The relaxation test, also known as the comb test, will allow you to determine when the hair is relaxed to the desired degree or whether additional smoothing is required.

>> It is essential that the hair is thoroughly rinsed to make sure that all relaxer product is removed from the hair prior to neutralizing.

>> Blotting removes excess water so that the neutralizing process is not adversely affected. It also gives you the opportunity to carefully check for any chemicals that have not been rinsed.

>> The acid-balanced neutralizer (shampoo or stabilizer) rehardens (locks) the hair into its new, straighter shape and restores the broken disulfide bonds.

RELAXER
GUEST EXPERIENCE // 111ᶜ.15

EXPLORE //

Have you ever had a salon professional who provided great technical skills, but "dropped the ball" when it came to everything else the service involved? Did this experience make you want to return to that stylist or salon?

INSPIRE //

Creating an exceptional guest experience greatly increases the value of your technical relaxing skills to your clients. As trust builds between you and your client, they become a repeat client who is glad to refer you to family and friends.

ACHIEVE //

Following this lesson on *Relaxer Guest Experience*, you'll be able to:

>> Summarize the service essentials related to relaxer services

>> Provide examples of infection control and safety guidelines for relaxer services

FOCUS //

RELAXER GUEST EXPERIENCE

Relaxer Service Essentials

Relaxer Infection Control and Safety

In a salon environment, the guest experience relates to your communication, consultation and after-care advice. As with all hair services, communication with your client prior to the relaxer service will ensure predictable results and will help you avoid any misunderstanding.

111°.15 | RELAXER GUEST EXPERIENCE

Before applying any relaxer chemicals to the hair, it's necessary to have a thorough consultation with the client. Success comes from listening carefully and recording all the important information in the chemical record. One of the most important considerations for a successful service is being sure you understand the new texture pattern your client desires. You will also ask questions to determine past and current products used on the hair.

►► RELAXER SERVICE ESSENTIALS

A client release statement helps the school or salon owner avoid retribution as a result of any damages or accidents and may be required as part of some malpractice insurance policies.

>> It is not a legal document.

>> It may not absolve the hairstylist from responsibility for damage that may occur to the client's hair as a result of the chemical service.

CLIENT CHEMICAL REFORMATION/RELAXER RECORD

Date	Wrap	Rod Size	Products	Process Time	Results
			Booster		☐ Good
					☐ Poor
					☐ Too Tight
			Reformation		☐ Too Loose
					Remarks:

Description of Hair:

Length	Density	Texture	Porosity	Elasticity	Test Curl Results
• Short	• Light	• Fine	• Average	• Good	• Negative
• Medium	• Medium	• Medium	• Resistant	• Normal	• Positive
• Long	• Heavy	• Coarse	• Extreme Porosity	• Poor	

Medications: _____

Vitamins: _____

Comments: _____

_____

Price of Service: $_____

Signature of Student: _____   Signature of Instructor: _____

_____   _____

CLIENT CHEMICAL REFORMATION/RELAXER RELEASE FORM

Name: _____   Phone Number: _____

Address: _____   City, State, Postal Code: _____

I request a relaxer and I fully understand that this service is to be given by a student of cosmetology at Your Name Beauty School. I hereby express my willingness for a student to do this work. I furthermore understand that I will assume full responsibility thereof.

Your Name Beauty School

Witness: _____   Client Signature: _____

Date: _____   Date: _____

To make the proper decisions for a successful relaxer service, ask your client open-ended questions to determine:

» Their preferred way of styling and wearing their hair on a regular basis

» How much of the existing texture they would like reduced

» The complete history of their past chemical services, including any problems they may have had

» Any fears, worries or misconceptions they may be concerned with

As you review the four Service Essentials, remember the impact of active listening, critical thinking and analysis on the overall success of the service. Pay attention to the following guidelines as you perform the relaxer service.

CONNECT

» Meet and greet the client with a firm handshake and pleasant tone of voice.

» Communicate to build rapport and develop a connection with the client.

CONSULT

» Help your client fill out a consultation form.

» Ask questions to discover the client's wants and needs:
   ▪ How much curl or texture does the client want reduced?
   ▪ Use photos or a styling guide for clear communication.

» Check into your client's relaxer history:
   ▪ Have there been problems with relaxers used in the past?
   ▪ Are there particular details that your client would like to share about their hair, such as breakage, thinning, etc.?

» Analyze your client's:
   ▪ Face and body shape
   ▪ Physical features
   ▪ Lifestyle
   ▪ Climate effects
   ▪ Hair and scalp type
   ▪ Hair condition

» Assess the facts and thoroughly think through your recommendations.

» Document everything that is important to the successful outcome of this service and future services.

» Ask client to sign the release form, which is required by some malpractice insurance companies. This standard release form states that the school or salon is not responsible for damages that may occur.

» Explain your recommended solutions as well as the price for the service(s).

» Focus on the physical and emotional needs of your client, building rapport and clarifying communication. Reinforce what you began in the Connect service essential if your client is hesitant with your recommendations.

» Gain feedback from your client and obtain consent before proceeding with the service.

CREATE

» Ensure client protection by draping with a plastic cape and towel.

» Ensure client comfort throughout service.

» Deliver all steps of the relaxer service to the best of your ability.

» Teach client how to perform home hair-care maintenance to keep the hair healthy and maintain the overall look of the new style with the relaxed texture.

COMPLETE

» Request specific feedback from client; ask questions and look for verbal and nonverbal cues to determine client satisfaction.

» Recommend products to maintain the healthy condition of your client's hair and scalp.

» Suggest a follow-up appointment and time frame for your client's next visit.

» Accompany client to the reception/ payment area or to the door; send client off with a warm goodbye.

» Complete the record with accurate information for future services.

SALON**CONNECTION**

Know Your Client's Chemical History

Relaxers can be performed on different types of curl patterns. Even clients with only a slight wave pattern might request a relaxer if they want straighter hair. Remember—products that contain ammonium thioglycolate are not only thio *relaxers*, they are also traditional *perms*. So, be aware of *all* services your client has received. The length of time you need to know about correlates to the length of their hair.

This means, if their hair is 7" long, you need to know what they've done for the last 14 months (since hair grows on average a half-inch per month). A client may not think a perm they received a year ago is important, but you need a complete history to ensure that you choose the appropriate relaxer product.

COMMUNICATION GUIDELINES

The examples presented here will help make you aware of things clients might say during a relaxer service and how to respond in ways that encourage open communication. Listen to what your clients say, watch their body language and respond to each individual client with empathy and respect.

CLIENT CUE	DESIGNER RESPONSE
"My hairline is tingling."	"Where do you feel the tingling? I'm going to use a damp towel to gently wipe off some of the relaxer product that has gotten onto your skin. Let me know right away if you feel the tingling again."
"May I have a 'perm'?"	"Do you want more wave or curl in your hair, or do you want to reduce the amount of curl? Tell me more about what kind of look you want so I can determine the appropriate service for you."
"Can I still straighten my hair if I have breakage?"	"Do you ever chemically straighten your hair at home? How often, if at all do you use thermal styling tools on your hair?" "If I determine it's safe to perform a relaxer service I can customize it by applying a gentler strength around your hairline and where your hair density is finer if needed." "If I determine that there is too much breakage, it's best if we don't proceed with the relaxer service. Instead, we can do a conditioning treatment and a finished style with a more relaxed look. We can consider a relaxer service when the breakage has grown out."
"Since my last relaxer service, my hair doesn't hold a set anymore."	"It appears your hair is somewhat over-processed and I would advise against doing a relaxer service today. Let's condition and trim your hair instead. When you have enough new growth, we can consider a relaxer service at that time."
"I was told that I can't color my hair if I relax it. Is that true?"	"Not entirely. We can use temporary or semi-permanent colors right after the relaxer service to add tone or shine. As long as your hair is in good condition, we can use permanent color 10-14 days after your relaxer service. In 2-3 weeks we can use a permanent color that slightly lightens your natural color as well. The only thing that is not recommended is using lightener on relaxed hair."
"How can I keep my relaxed hair looking great?"	"Here are some simple at-home tips: 1. Use moisture-based shampoos, conditioners and styling products. 2. Use silicone-based products (creams, pomades, etc.) to keep hair manageable and shiny. 3. Avoid using excess heat and/or pulling the hair when styling at home. 4. Return to the salon for regular trims, conditioning and styling services to keep your hair in tip-top shape."

► RELAXER INFECTION CONTROL AND SAFETY

It is your responsibility to protect your client by following infection control and safety guidelines with any and all services you provide.

Cleaning is a process of removing dirt, debris and potential pathogens to aid in slowing the growth of pathogens. Cleaning is performed prior to disinfection procedures.

Disinfection methods kill certain pathogens (bacteria, viruses and fungi) with the exception of spores. Disinfectants are available in varied forms, including concentrate, liquid, spray or wipes that are approved EPA-registered disinfectants available for use in the salon industry. Immersion, and the use of disinfecting spray or wipes are common practices when it comes to disinfecting tools, multi-use supplies and equipment in the salon. Be sure to follow the manufacturer's directions for mixing disinfecting solutions and contact time, if applicable.

SAFETY PRECAUTIONS

1. Practice infection control guidelines. Wash your hands.

2. Protect yourself. Wear gloves when applying chemical solutions.

3. Protect your client's clothing with proper draping. See "Draping for Chemical Services" in the *Perm Guest Experience* lesson.

4. Check the scalp for abrasions or diseases. Do not proceed with relaxer services if abrasions or diseases are present. Postpone and reschedule the relaxer service until the scalp is healthy again.

5. Advise client not to shampoo within 48 hours prior to a sodium hydroxide relaxer service. The natural oils protect the scalp when performing the service. Shampoo the client's hair lightly prior to an ammonium thioglycolate relaxer service.

6. Perform a strand test to determine hair's competency. If the hair is dry, brittle or overporous, recondition it first and/or cut off damaged ends to avoid overprocessing. See "Preliminary Strand Test" in this lesson.

7. Perform a test for metallic salts if there is a possibility that such a product is on the hair. See "Test for Metallic Salts" in the *Perm Guest Experience* lesson.

8. Avoid brushing or pulling the hair before giving any chemical service to prevent scalp irritation.

9. Never use sodium hydroxide to relax hair that has been treated with a thio product or vice versa. The results could be severe breakage and/or irreversible damage.

10. Take special care with lightened (bleached) hair. Most lightened hair is unable to receive relaxer services.

11. Apply base cream around the hairline and ears to prevent skin irritation when performing all relaxer services.

12. If a client experiences burning during a sodium hydroxide relaxer service, rinse the hair with warm water, apply neutralizing shampoo and proceed with remaining service.

13. Perform several strand tests to avoid overprocessing.

14. Follow the manufacturer's directions. Do not dilute or add anything to the solution or the neutralizer unless indicated by the manufacturer's instructions. Monitor timing guidelines closely.

15. Avoid chemical burns and irritation to the skin, eyes and nose by keeping all products away from them. If chemicals accidently get on the skin, flush the area with cool water. If product gets into the eyes, flush them thoroughly with lukewarm water and consult a physician immediately.

16. Secure cotton strips around the hairline before applying neutralizer to keep it off the skin. When the cotton becomes wet, replace it immediately. For added protection (optional), place a neutralizing bib around the hairline with the elastic bands on top of the cotton to prevent skin irritation or chemical burns when rinsing.

DRAPING FOR CHEMICAL SERVICES

Proper draping procedures for relaxer services are very important. Draping protects client's clothing and helps prevent skin irritation or burns

When draping your client for a chemical service, place a towel under the plastic cape and another towel on top. Refer to the *Perm Guest Experience* lesson for details on this draping procedure.

SCALP ANALYSIS

Relaxers involve the use of strong chemicals, so examine and analyze the condition of your client's scalp before the service in order to ensure client safety. When the scalp is healthy, you may proceed with the service, provided the hair is structurally competent. Look for any abnormalities on the scalp such as:

>> Cuts
>> Scratches
>> Sores
>> Abrasions

If you find any of these irregularities, postpone the relaxer service until the scalp is healthy again. **Never apply chemicals over any abnormal scalp condition.** To do so could cause chemical burns and scalp problems.

You may need to conduct several preliminary tests before a relaxer service to gain an accurate assessment of the client's hair to ensure successful results. As you perform these tests, carefully analyze the condition of the hair and scalp. If you see signs of breakage in the hair or abrasions and irritations on the scalp, postpone the service until the condition improves. Refer to the *Relaxer Skills* lesson and the "Safety Precautions" portion of this lesson for additional information on how to assess hair for a relaxer service.

PRELIMINARY STRAND TEST

Strand testing evaluates the overall condition of the hair to determine if it can withstand the relaxer service. To perform a strand test:

>> Part off a small section of hair in the most resistant area of the head

>> Apply the chemical relaxer to the test strand

>> Follow the manufacturer's timing guide and check the test area frequently

>> Smooth the hair to straighten it

>> Rinse, then use a neutralizing shampoo and towel-dry the test area thoroughly

>> Test in another area using a stronger relaxer strength if the test strands did not relax enough

TEST FOR METALLIC SALTS

Color products that restore color or progressively darken the hair (sometimes called hair restorers) contain metallic salts. These form a residue on the hair that interferes with the chemical action. Performing a chemical service on hair with metallic salts can result in:

>> Uneven texture

>> Distinct discoloration

>> Hair damage

>> Breakage

To avoid such negative results perform a test for metallic salts, also called a 1:20 test, before performing a relaxer service. Review the *Perm Guest Experience* lesson for details on testing for metallic salts.

CLEANING AND DISINFECTION GUIDELINES

Keep in mind that only nonporous tools, supplies and equipment can be disinfected. All single-use items must be discarded after each use. Always follow your area's regulatory guidelines.

TOOLS, SUPPLIES AND EQUIPMENT	CLEANING GUIDELINES	DISINFECTION GUIDELINES
Bowl	» Preclean with soap and water.	» Use an approved EPA-registered disinfectant solution, wipe or spray.
Applicator Brush	» Remove hair and debris. » Preclean with soap and water. » Dry thoroughly.	» Use an approved EPA-registered disinfectant solution, wipe or spray.
Tail Comb (non-metal)	» Remove hair and debris. » Preclean with soap and water.	» Immerse in an approved EPA-registered disinfectant solution.
Shampoo Comb	» Remove hair and debris. » Preclean with soap and water.	» Immerse in an approved EPA-registered disinfectant solution.
Sectioning Clips	» Preclean with soap and water.	» Immerse in an approved EPA-registered disinfectant solution.
Protective Cape	» Remove hair and chemical product from cape. » Wash in washing machine with soap after each use.	» Some regulatory agencies may require use of an approved EPA-registered disinfectant.
Cloth Towels	» Remove hair from towels. » Wash in washing machine with soap after each use.	» Some regulatory agencies may require use of an approved EPA-registered disinfectant.

Store disinfected tools and multi-use supplies in a clean, dry, covered container or cabinet.

 If tools, multi-use supplies or equipment have come in contact with blood or body fluids, the following disinfection procedures must take place: **Use an approved EPA-registered hospital disinfectant according to manufacturer's directions and as required by your area's regulatory agency.**

CARE AND SAFETY

Follow infection control procedures for personal care and client safety guidelines before and during the relaxer service to ensure your safety and the client's, while also contributing to the salon care.

Personal Care	Client Care Prior to the Service	Client Care During the Service	Salon Care
» Check that your personal standards of health and hygiene minimize the spread of infection.	» Protect the client's skin and clothing with a freshly laundered towel and a freshly laundered protective cape.	» If pre-shampooing is necessary, use light massage movements and tepid (lukewarm) water.	» Follow health and safety guidelines, including cleaning and disinfecting procedures.
» Wash hands and dry thoroughly with a single-use towel.	» Check the scalp for any diseases or disorders. If any are evident, refer client to a physician, do not proceed with the service.	» Protect the client's skin by applying base cream.	» Ensure equipment, including the salon chair, is clean and disinfected.
» Disinfect workstation.	» Perform a test for metallic salts if there is a possibility that such a product is on the hair.	» Do not permit the product to come in contact with the eyes. If it does, rinse the eyes immediately with tepid water.	» Promote a professional image by ensuring your workstation is clean and tidy throughout the service.
» Clean and disinfect tools appropriately.	» Analyze the client's hair to determine the correct product to use.	» Check in and ask client about any scalp sensitivity or irritations.	» Use disinfected applicator bottles, brushes and combs; use only plastic or glass bowls to hold relaxer.
» Protect yourself by wearing personal protective equipment such as gloves and an apron.	» Be sure the cape stays in place and the client's arms are underneath the cape.	» Monitor relaxer service and perform relaxation test as needed.	» Discard any leftover relaxer product once the service is complete.
» Refer to your regulatory agency for proper mixing/handling of disinfectant solutions.	» If any tools are dropped on the floor, pick them up then clean and disinfect.	» Disinfect workstation following the service.	» Refer to SDS (Safety Data Sheets).
» Minimize fatigue by maintaining good posture during the service.	» Update the client record noting hair/scalp condition.		» Complete the client record noting the formula, processing time, and any sensitivities experienced.

Remember that providing an exceptional guest experience is as important as your technical skills when it comes to satisfied clients prebooking return relaxer services.

LESSONS LEARNED

The service essentials related to a relaxer service can be summarized as follows:

>> Connect – Meet and greet clients and communicate to build rapport.

>> Consult – Ask questions to discover client needs and relaxer history; analyze client's face, body shape, physical features, hair and scalp; explain recommended solutions and gain feedback and obtain consent to move forward.

>> Create – Ensure client safety and comfort; stay focused to deliver the best service; explain process and products to your client; teach the client at-home care maintenance.

>> Complete – Request specific feedback; recommend home-care products; suggest future appointment times; complete client record.

Infection control and safety guidelines must be followed throughout a relaxer service to ensure your safety and the safety of the clients and the salon. Disinfectants are available in varied forms including concentrate, liquid, spray or wipes that have EPA approval for use in the salon industry. Be guided by your area's regulatory agency for proper cleaning and disinfection guidelines.

RELAXER SERVICE | 111ᶜ.16

EXPLORE // **Have you ever had a hair service that didn't turn out exactly the way you hoped? How can specific service procedures and guidelines help ensure consistent, predictable results?**

INSPIRE //

Performing a relaxer application with correct procedures before, during and after the service ensures the desired level of straightness is achieved.

ACHIEVE //

Following this lesson on *Relaxer Service*, you'll be able to:

>> Provide examples of procedural guidelines to follow when performing a relaxer service

>> Describe the three areas of a relaxer service

>> Restate solutions to common relaxer problems

FOCUS //

RELAXER SERVICE

Relaxer Client Guidelines

Relaxer Service Overview

Relaxer Problems and Solutions

Relaxer Rubric

Your specialized skills in providing chemical texture services will allow you to transform your clients' appearance, giving them the curly-to-straight looks they want while building your clientele and professional reputation.

111ᶜ.16 |
RELAXER SERVICE

Incorporating what you've learned about relaxer theory, tools, skills and guest relations and applying your knowledge to your relaxer services ensures client safety and satisfaction.

RELAXER CLIENT GUIDELINES

Client-centered guidelines help develop your chair-side manner. This builds trust and loyalty among your clients and leads to career success for you.

PROCEDURAL GUIDELINES

The following chart will ensure your client's comfort and safety during relaxer services.

SECTION	
	» Bring any current damage to client's attention. ▪ Ask questions to find out why breakage has occurred. » If client has been relaxing their own hair at home, discuss the risks of doing this. » Educate client on benefits of a professional relaxer service.
APPLY	
	» Watch for any product that might drip or fall as you apply it throughout the relaxer procedure. Change client's cape and towel as often as necessary. » Check with your area's regulatory agency for proper application procedures to use while you are in school. » As your experience grows, you may become proficient enough that you can apply product to only one side of the strand while still getting desired distribution and penetration of product.
COMB OR SMOOTH	
	» Ask client to inform you if they feel any scalp discomfort. » Be sure to connect all sections of the hair together while smoothing to avoid separation marks due to sectioning pattern.
TEST	
	» Do not leave client unattended. » Perform relaxation tests frequently to avoid overprocessing hair. » Rinse product out of hair immediately if you see the hair becoming limp or fragile during the relaxation test. » Rinse product thoroughly for 5-15 minutes once the desired level of relaxation is achieved. Check to ensure client's comfort during this time.
NEUTRALIZE	
	» Make sure hair remains straight while rinsing. » Assess condition of client's hair in order to choose the most appropriate finishing techniques and products.

RELAXER SERVICE OVERVIEW

The Relaxer Service Overview identifies the three areas of sodium hydroxide and ammonium thioglycolate relaxer services:

>> Relaxer Preparation provides a brief overview of the steps to follow *before* you actually begin the relaxer service.

>> Relaxer Procedure provides an overview of the procedures you will use *during* the relaxer service to ensure predictable results.

>> Relaxer Completion provides an overview of the steps to follow *after* performing the relaxer service to ensure guest satisfaction.

SERVICE ESSENTIALS: THE FOUR Cs
The relaxer procedures include attention to the four Cs.

1. **CONNECT**
   Establishes rapport and builds credibility with each client

2. **CONSULT**
   Analyzes client wants and needs, visualizes the end result, organizes the plan for follow-through and obtains client agreement

3. **CREATE**
   Produces functional, predictable and pleasing results

4. **COMPLETE**
   Reviews the service experience and client satisfaction, offers product recommendations, expresses appreciation and provides follow-up

RELAXER PREPARATION*

PREPARATION	>> Clean and disinfect workstation.
	>> Assemble relaxer essentials that include sectioning clips, non-metal tail comb, gloves, base cream, relaxer, bowl and applicator brush.
	>> Wash hands.
	>> Perform analysis of hair and scalp.
	>> Ask client to remove jewelry and store in a secure place.
	>> Perform preliminary strand test and elasticity test.
	>> Review previous client record if applicable.

* Preparation steps are the same for all relaxer procedures.

ALERT!
Never apply a thio relaxer over hair that has been relaxed with a sodium hydroxide relaxer or vice versa, since these two chemicals are not compatible. Severe damage and breakage can occur.

SODIUM HYDROXIDE RELAXER PROCEDURE*

Sodium hydroxide relaxers can be used to permanently straighten any type of hair but are especially designed for tightly curled hair. A sodium hydroxide relaxer is a progressive product. Once applied, the hair cannot return to its original state, and a thio relaxer service cannot be performed afterward.

PROCEDURE	
	>> Drape client for chemical service.
	>> Product is first applied to most resistant area ¼" (.6 cm) to ½" (1.25 cm) away from the scalp to porous ends.
	>> Partings should be approximately ¼" (.6 cm).
	>> Product should be applied to both sides of the strand.
	>> Heat from the scalp will cause the product to spread toward the scalp. However, if necessary, apply product closer to the scalp:
	▪ Do so only after you have first applied it midstrand throughout.
	▪ Never apply product directly to the scalp.
	>> Apply the relaxer to the perimeter hairline last, since the hairline is sensitive to breakage and usually finer in texture.

OPTIONAL PROCEDURE	
	The application procedure is a guideline. Other application techniques are also acceptable. For example:
	>> You may begin the application at the ridge of the first curl.
	>> To equalize processing time on long hair, you may begin the application farther away from the scalp to avoid overprocessing the hair.

* For Preparation and Completion steps, see pages 171 and 175 respectively.

VIRGIN SODIUM HYDROXIDE RELAXER PROCEDURE*

PROCEDURE	
	>> Drape client for chemical service.
	>> DO NOT pre-shampoo the client's hair.
	>> **Section** hair into five sections.
	>> **Apply** base cream around hairline, top of ears and scalp of each section.
	▪ Use checkerboard technique.
	▪ Use ¼" (.6 cm) to ½" (1.25 cm) horizontal and vertical partings
	>> Apply relaxer starting at top of back-right section using ¼" (.6 cm) horizontal partings, applying ½" (1.25 cm) away from base through midstrand, avoiding ends.
	>> Apply to top and bottom of parting; work toward bottom of section; bring lengths down; work from the back to the sides to the top, using diagonal-back partings at the sides and horizontal partings at the top.
	▪ Avoid touching scalp.
	▪ Follow the same pattern when applying to the base and ends; do not apply directly to scalp.
	▪ Apply relaxer to entire hairline starting at front hairline and working toward nape on both sides.
	>> **Smooth** top and bottom of each ¼" (.6 cm) parting, starting at top of back-right section.
	▪ Smooth from base to ends using back of comb.
	▪ Bring lengths down.
	▪ Work from back to the sides to the top.
	>> Perform a comb relaxation **test** using spine or tail of comb.
	>> Rinse thoroughly and **neutralize** according to manufacturer's directions.
	>> Finish texture design.

* For Preparation and Completion steps, see pages 171 and 175 respectively.

RETOUCH SODIUM HYDROXIDE RELAXER PROCEDURE*

- » Drape client for chemical service.
- » DO NOT pre-shampoo the hair.
- » **Section** the hair into 5 sections.
- » Apply base cream around hairline, tops of ears and scalp of each section.
  - ▪ Use checkerboard technique.
  - ▪ Use ¼" (.6 cm) to ½" (1.25 cm) horizontal and vertical partings.
- » Apply protective cream to previously relaxed hair.
  - ▪ Start at top of back-right section.
  - ▪ Apply to top and then bottom of ½" (1.25 cm) horizontal partings from line of demarcation to ends.
  - ▪ Work from back to sides to the top of the head.
- » **Apply** relaxer starting at top of back-right section.
  - ▪ Use ¼" (.6 cm) horizontal partings.
  - ▪ Apply to top and bottom of new growth area only.
  - ▪ Avoid touching the scalp.
- » Work from the back to the sides to the top, using diagonal-back partings at the sides and horizontal partings at the top.
  - ▪ Avoid applying to the hairline.
  - ▪ Bring lengths down.
- » Apply relaxer to entire hairline, starting at front hairline and working toward nape hairline on both sides.
- » **Smooth** top and bottom of ¼" (.6 cm) partings in new growth area.
  - ▪ Start in top of back-right section using back of comb.
  - ▪ Bring lengths down.
  - ▪ Work from the back to the sides to the top of the head.
- » Perform a curl relaxation **test** using spine or tail of comb.
- » Rinse thoroughly and **neutralize** according to manufacturer's directions.
- » Finish texture design.

The application procedure is a guideline. Other application techniques are also acceptable. For example:
- » You may begin the application at the ridge of the first curl.
- » Your instructor may also have additional guidelines.

* For Preparation and Completion steps, see pages 171 and 175 respectively.

DISCOVER**MORE**

All hair does not relax the same way. Research online to learn about the differences between relaxer strengths and why it's so important to choose the appropriate strength. Discover what it is that makes a mild strength relaxer process slower than a super strength relaxer.

AMMONIUM THIOGLYCOLATE RELAXER PROCEDURE*

PROCEDURE

>> The first-time application is applied to the most resistant area and ¼" (.6 cm) to ½" (1.25 cm) away from the scalp out to the porous ends.

>> Additional product may then be applied at the base (scalp area) if necessary.

>> **Product is applied to the base last, since the hair near the scalp will process more quickly due to body heat.**

>> A non-alkaline shampoo is recommended after the chemical relaxer has been rinsed from the hair.

>> Natural oils that are removed during the chemical relaxing process are replaced with a conditioning treatment.

* For Preparation and Completion steps, see pages 171 and 175 respectively.

VIRGIN AMMONIUM THIOGLYCOLATE RELAXER PROCEDURE*

PROCEDURE

>> Drape client for chemical service.

>> Pre-shampoo the hair lightly.

>> **Section** the hair into 5 sections.

>> Apply base cream around hairline and tops of ears.

>> **Apply** relaxer starting at top of back-right section, using ¼" (.6 cm) horizontal partings and applying ½" (1.25 cm) from base through midstrand, avoiding ends.

>> Apply relaxer to top and bottom of each parting; work toward bottom of section; bring lengths down.

>> Work from the back to the sides to the top, using diagonal-back partings at the sides and horizontal partings at the top.

>> Apply relaxer to the base and porous ends in each section using same parting pattern and technique; avoid touching scalp.

>> **Smooth** top and bottom of each ¼" (.6 cm) parting, starting at top of back-right section from base to ends using back of comb; bring lengths down; work from back to sides to top.

>> Perform a comb relaxation **test** using spine or tail of comb.

>> Rinse thoroughly and **neutralize** according to manufacturer's directions.

>> Finish texture design.

* For Preparation and Completion steps, see pages 171 and 175 respectively.

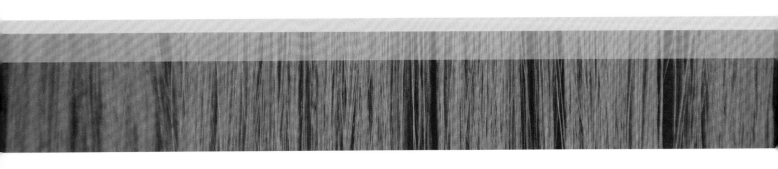

RETOUCH AMMONIUM THIOGLYCOLATE PROCEDURE*

PROCEDURE

>> Drape client for chemical service.
>> Pre-shampoo the hair lightly.
>> **Section** hair into 5 sections.
>> Apply base cream around entire hairline and top of ears.
>> Apply protective cream to previously relaxed hair starting at top of back-right section; use ½" (1.25 cm) horizontal partings, applying to top and then bottom of each parting from line of demarcation to ends; apply protective cream to remaining sections using same technique.
>> **Apply** relaxer first, outlining back-right section (avoiding nape hairline), and then apply to top and bottom of ¼" (.6 cm) horizontal partings in new growth area only; avoid touching scalp; bring lengths down; work from back to sides to top, using diagonal-back partings on the sides and horizontal partings at the top.
>> **Smooth** top and bottom of ¼" (.6 cm) partings in new growth area, starting at top of back-right section using back of comb; bring lengths down; work from back to sides to top.
>> Perform comb relaxation **test** using spine or tail of comb.
>> Rinse thoroughly and **neutralize** according to manufacturer's directions.
>> Finish texture design.

* For Preparation and Completion steps, see page 171 and below, respectively.

RELAXER COMPLETION*

COMPLETION

>> Reinforce client's satisfaction with their overall experience.
>> Make professional product recommendations.
>> Prebook client's next appointment.
>> End client's visit with warm and personable goodbye.
>> Discard single-use materials; disinfect tools and multi-use supplies; disinfect workstation and arrange in proper order.
>> Wash hands.
>> Complete client record.

* Completion steps are the same for all relaxer procedures.

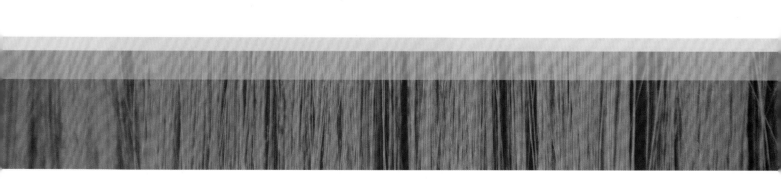

RELAXER PROBLEMS AND SOLUTIONS

Following are a few problems that may occur with relaxers, along with their possible causes and solutions.

EXTREME BREAKAGE SHORTLY AFTER RELAXING

Cause: Improper neutralizing allows active ingredients to remain in the hairstrand

Solution: Allow the neutralizer product to remain in the hair no longer than specified in manufacturer's directions and ensure neutralizer is thoroughly rinsed.

BREAKAGE WITHIN THE NAPE AFTER RELAXING

Cause: Overprocessing; relaxer product left in the neck of the shampoo bowl comes in contact with client's nape when client leans back into bowl after rinsing product from hair

Solution: Rinse the relaxer from the neck of the bowl before leaning client back into the bowl after rinsing product from the hair.

IRRITATION OR SENSITIVITY AROUND THE HAIRLINE

Cause: Client cleansed their face and extended cleansing into the hairline before the relaxer service

Solution: Instruct clients to avoid cleansing into the hairline prior to the service.

RELAXER RUBRIC

A performance rubric is a document that identifies criteria at which levels of performance can be measured objectively. The Relaxer Rubric is an example that an instructor might choose to use for scoring. The Relaxer Rubric is divided into three main areas— Preparation, Procedure and Completion. Each area is further divided into step-by-step procedures that will ensure client safety and satisfaction.

RELAXER RUBRIC

Student Name: _____ ID Number: _____

Instructor: _____ Date: _____ Start Time: _____ End Time: _____

RELAXER (Live Model) – Each scoring item is marked with either a "Yes" or "No." Each "Yes" counts for one point. Total number of points attainable is 34.

CRITERIA	YES	NO	INSTRUCTOR ASSESSMENT
PREPARATION: Did student...			
1. Set up workstation with properly labeled supplies?	☐	☐	
2. Place disinfected tools and supplies at a visibly clean workstation?	☐	☐	
3. Wash hands?	☐	☐	
Connect: Did student...			
4. Meet and greet client with a welcoming smile and pleasant tone of voice?	☐	☐	
5. Communicate to build rapport and develop a relationship with client?	☐	☐	
6. Refer to client by name throughout service?	☐	☐	
Consult: Did student...			
7. Ask questions to discover client's wants and needs?	☐	☐	
8. Analyze client's hair and scalp and check for any contraindications?	☐	☐	
9. Gain feedback and consent from client before proceeding?	☐	☐	
PROCEDURE: Did student...			
10. Properly drape client and prepare for service?	☐	☐	
11. Ensure client protection and comfort by maintaining cape on outside of chair at all times?	☐	☐	
12. Carry out appropriate shampoo and condition procedures when applicable?	☐	☐	
13. Use products and supplies economically?	☐	☐	
Create: Did student...			
14. Section the hair into 5 sections for control?	☐	☐	
15. Apply base cream around entire hairline and tops of ears and use the checkerboard technique if needed?	☐	☐	
16. Select correct relaxer strength for the desired result?	☐	☐	
17. Part the hair for the application methods and relaxer service performed?	☐	☐	
18. Apply relaxer appropriately to the hair?	☐	☐	
19. Use relaxer tools and supplies accurately and efficiently throughout application?	☐	☐	
20. Smooth the top and bottom of partings to achieve desired result?	☐	☐	
21. Process relaxer according to manufacturer's directions?	☐	☐	
22. Perform comb relaxation test using spine or tail of comb?	☐	☐	
23. Rinse and neutralize following manufacturer's directions?	☐	☐	
24. Teach client to use products to maintain the appearance and condition of the hair?	☐	☐	
25. Practice infection control procedures and safety guidelines throughout service?	☐	☐	
COMPLETION (Complete): Did student...			
26. Ask questions and look for verbal and nonverbal cues to determine client's level of satisfaction?	☐	☐	
27. Make professional product recommendations?	☐	☐	
28. Ask client to make a future appointment?	☐	☐	
29. End client's visit with a warm and personal goodbye?	☐	☐	
30. Discard single-use supplies?	☐	☐	
31. Disinfect tools and multi-use supplies; disinfect workstation and arrange in proper order?	☐	☐	
32. Complete service within scheduled time?	☐	☐	
33. Complete client record?	☐	☐	
34. Wash their hands following service?	☐	☐	

COMMENTS: _____ TOTAL POINTS = _____ ÷ 34 = _____ %

Each of the procedural steps used to apply relaxer product affects the service results, as well as your client's safety. Consistently achieving predictable results while build a loyal clientele.

LESSONS LEARNED

Procedural guidelines to follow when performing a relaxer service to ensure client safety include:

>> Sectioning the hair for control, speed and accuracy when applying the relaxer product

>> Using consistent partings to ensure proper penetration of product for more even results

>> Applying product neatly and accurately; avoiding product application on the skin or overlapping product onto previously relaxed hair (retouch), which could cause breakage

>> Processing the relaxer according to manufacturer's directions to avoid overprocessing

>> Performing comb relaxation tests to ensure the desired level of straightness is achieved

>> Rinsing thoroughly and neutralizing to lock the hair into its new straight shape

The three areas of a relaxer service include the Preparation, Procedure and Completion:

>> Preparation – Includes setting up the workstation, disinfected tools and supplies; connecting with client and properly draping the client

>> Procedure – Includes ensuring client safety, performing the relaxer service, neutralizing the hair and sufficiently rinsing all chemicals

>> Completion – Includes infection control and safety procedures, such as discarding non-reusable materials, arranging/disinfecting workstation, determining client's level of satisfaction, recommending products, asking client to prebook a future appointment, ending client's visit with a warm and personal goodbye and completing the chemical client record

Proper hair analysis and thorough rinsing once relaxer product and neutralizer have been processed accordingly can prevent many problems in hair relaxer services.

VIRGIN THIO RELAXER

EXPLORE

Could you believe a service you provide could actually change a client's attitude toward their own hair?

INSPIRE

Clients with wavy or curly hair often want straighter, more manageable options. This virgin thio relaxer service will allow you to offer your clients a variety of options.

ACHIEVE

Following this *Virgin Thio Relaxer Workshop*, you'll be able to:

>> Identify the relaxer procedures related to the virgin thio relaxer

>> Create a repetition of smooth, straight texture on uniform lengths, using consistent ¼" (.6 cm) horizontal and diagonal-back partings

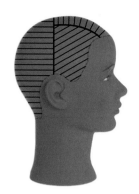

The finished relaxer design shows smooth, straight texture on uniformly layered lengths. The hair can be finished with a large-barrel thermal iron, set on low heat.

The head is sectioned into 5 sections. One-quarter inch (.6 cm) thick horizontal and diagonal-back partings are used to apply the relaxer product and smooth the lengths.

RELAXER PROCEDURES

1. SECTION

2. APPLY

3. COMB OR SMOOTH

4. TEST

5 . NEUTRALIZE

DESIGN DECISIONS CHART

VIRGIN THIO RELAXER

Draw or fill in the boxes with the appropriate answers.

DESIGN DECISIONS

EXISTING TEXTURE

☐ ☐ ☐

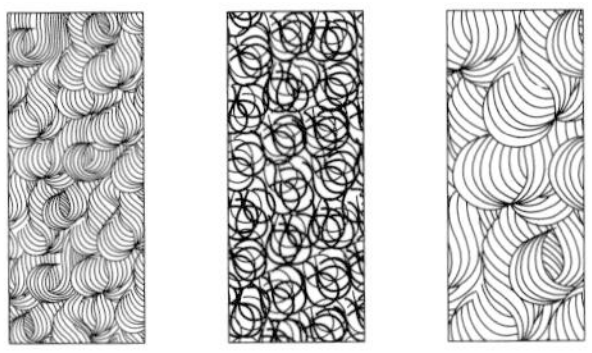

DESIRED TEXTURE

☐ ☐

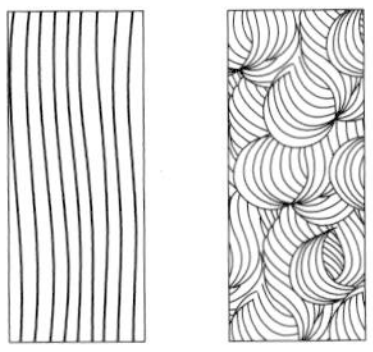

PRODUCT PLACEMENT

STRAND

☐ ☐

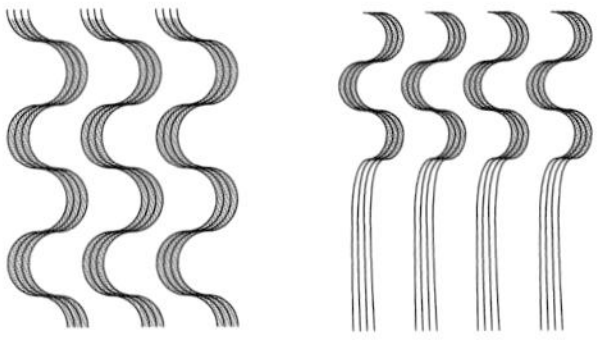

SECTIONING/PARTING PATTERN

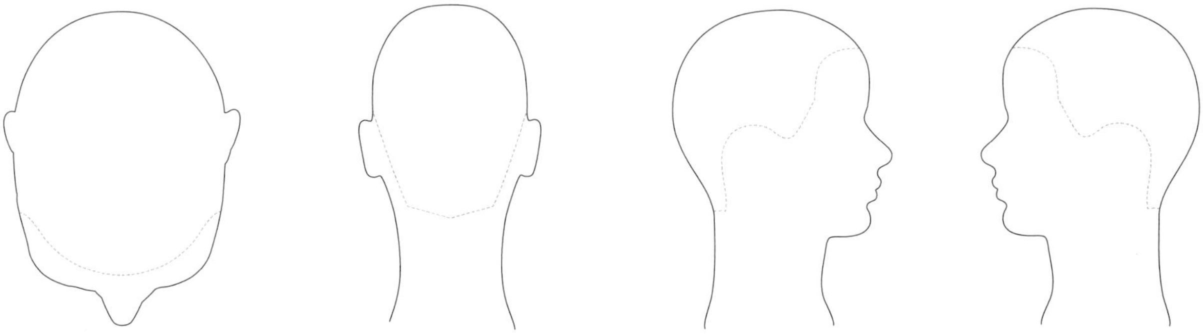

TOOL/PRODUCT CHOICE

____

____

____

Instructor Signature ______________________________ **Date** ______________

PERFORMANCE GUIDE

VIRGIN THIO RELAXER

View the video, complete the Design Decisions chart, then perform this workshop. Complete the self-check as you progress through the workshop.

3.5 mins
Suggested Salon Speed

PREPARATION		✔
	>> Assemble tools and products >> Set up workstation >> Shampoo hair **Note:** Do not condition.	☐

SECTION/APPLY BASE

	1. **Apply base cream:** >> Entire hairline >> Tops of ears	☐

APPLY – AWAY FROM BASE THROUGH MIDSTRAND

	2. **Begin relaxer application at top of right-back section:** >> ¼" (.6 cm) thick horizontal partings >> Apply ½" (1.25 cm) from base through midstrand; not to ends >> Apply to top, then bottom of each parting >> Gently place hair upward and out of the way	☐
	3. **Work toward bottom of section:** >> Repeat application to top and bottom of each parting >> Gently bring lengths down when section is complete	☐

4. **Move to back-left section:**
   - Apply relaxer using same technique
   - Bring lengths down when section is complete

5. **Move to left side in front of ear:**
   - ¼" (.6 cm) thick diagonal-back partings
   - Start at top of section

6. **Apply with same technique:**
   - Apply ½" (1.25 cm) away from base through midstrand; not to ends
   - Bring lengths down when section is complete

7. **Move to right side:**
   - Use same technique to apply
   - Work from top to bottom of section

8. **Apply to top section:**
   - Start at back of section
   - Apply first to bottom of each parting, directing hair toward front
   - Then apply to top of parting
   - Direct and position hair away from face
   - When section completed, place lengths off to one side before proceeding

APPLY – BASE AND POROUS ENDS ✔

9. **Return to first section:**
   >> Again, use ¼" (.6 cm) horizontal partings
   >> Apply relaxer to base, from scalp but not directly to scalp
   >> Then apply to porous ends
   >> Place each parting up and out of the way

10. **Bring lengths down when you complete section.**

11. **Apply to back-left section:**
    >> Apply relaxer to base and ends

12. **Apply to sides:**
    >> Start with left side
    >> ¼" (.6 cm) diagonal-back partings
    >> Apply to base and ends

13. **Move to right side:**
    >> Repeat same technique on this side

14. Apply to top section:

>> Work from back to front, applying to base and ends
>> Apply to bottom then top of partings
>> Keep hair out of face

SMOOTH

15. Smooth back sections:

>> Start on back-right side using ¼" (.6 cm) partings
>> Smooth each parting with back of tail comb
>> Smooth top of strand first, resting strand on palm of hand
>> Then smooth bottom of each parting, resting strand on palm
>> Direct partings upward
>> Work to bottom of section
>> Bring lengths down when completed
>> Repeat on left-back section

16. Smooth side sections:

>> Start on left side using ¼" (.6 cm) diagonal-back partings
>> Start at top of section and smooth
>> Bring lengths down when section is complete
>> Repeat on right side

17. Move to top section:

>> Work from back toward front
>> Smooth bottom and then top
>> Rest strand in your palm

Optional: You may work with the strand flat against the head in this or other areas.

TEST/NEUTRALIZE ✔

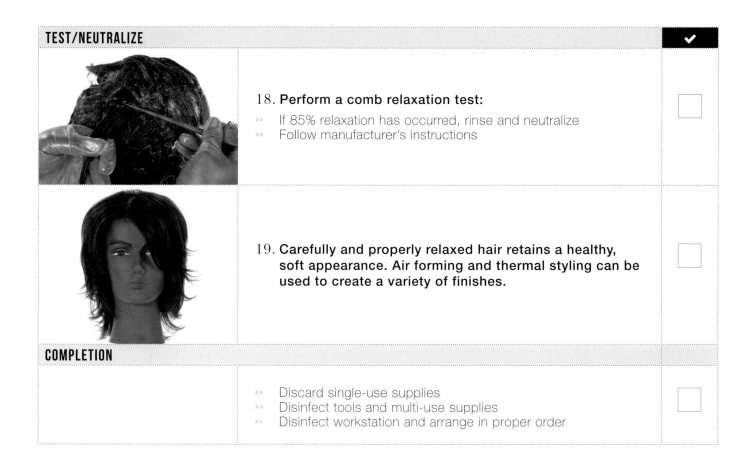

18. Perform a comb relaxation test:
>> If 85% relaxation has occurred, rinse and neutralize
>> Follow manufacturer's instructions

☐

19. Carefully and properly relaxed hair retains a healthy, soft appearance. Air forming and thermal styling can be used to create a variety of finishes.

☐

COMPLETION

>> Discard single-use supplies
>> Disinfect tools and multi-use supplies
>> Disinfect workstation and arrange in proper order

☐

35 mins
Suggested Salon Speed

My Speed
_____
_____
_____

INSTRUCTIONS:
Record your time in comparison with the suggested salon speed. Then, list here how you could improve your performance.

_____
_____
_____
_____
_____

VIRGIN SODIUM HYDROXIDE RELAXER

EXPLORE

What client would benefit from a sodium hydroxide service?

INSPIRE

Many clients with curly to tightly curled hair will want smoother, more manageable options. This service will help you give your clients a variety of options.

ACHIEVE

Following this *Virgin Sodium Hydroxide Relaxer Workshop*, you'll be able to:

>> Identify the relaxer procedures related to the virgin sodium hydroxide relaxer

>> Chemically relax natural curly hair to create a repetition of smooth, straight texture

The finished relaxer design shows a straight, soft appearance from base to ends.

The head is sectioned into 5 sections. One-quarter inch (.6 cm) horizontal and diagonal-back partings are used to apply the relaxer product.

RELAXER PROCEDURES

1. SECTION

2. APPLY

3. COMB OR SMOOTH

4. TEST

5. NEUTRALIZE

DESIGN DECISIONS CHART

VIRGIN SODIUM HYDROXIDE RELAXER

Draw or fill in the boxes with the appropriate answers.

DESIGN DECISIONS

EXISTING TEXTURE

☐ ☐ ☐

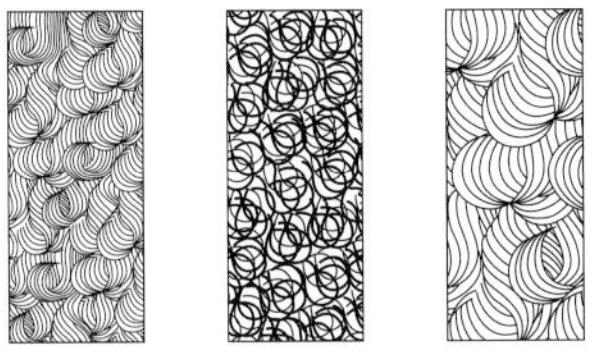

DESIRED TEXTURE

☐ ☐

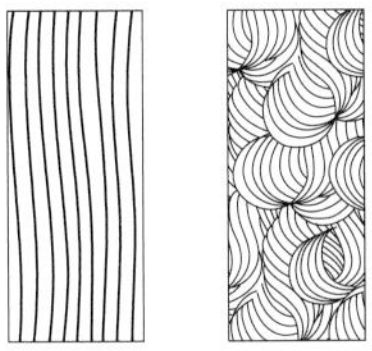

PRODUCT PLACEMENT

STRAND

☐ ☐

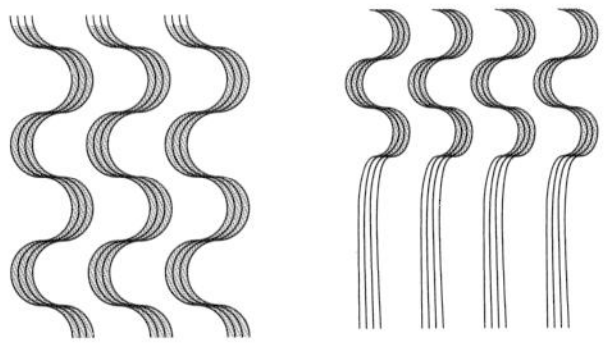

SECTIONING/PARTING PATTERN

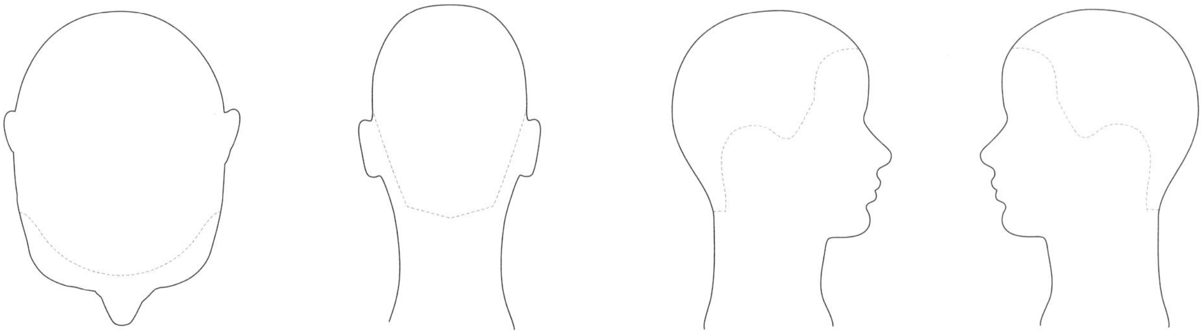

TOOL/PRODUCT CHOICE

____

____

____

Instructor Signature ________________________ **Date** ____________

PERFORMANCE GUIDE

VIRGIN SODIUM HYDROXIDE RELAXER

View the video, complete the Design Decisions chart, then perform this workshop. Complete the self-check as you progress through the workshop.

40 mins
Suggested
Salon Speed

PREPARATION	✔
>> Assemble tools and products >> Set up workstation	☐

HAIR PREPARATION – HAIR AND SCALP ANALYSIS

1. **Analyze hair:** >> Determine texture, density, porosity and overall quality of hair **Note:** Hair must not be shampooed prior to the sodium hydroxide relaxer service.	☐
2. **Perform scalp analysis:** >> Use tail comb to part through hair and examine >> Avoid touching scalp with tail comb to avoid potential scalp irritations	☐

SECTION/APPLY – BASE CREAM

3. **Section head into 5 sections:** >> Apex to center nape >> Ear to ear >> Rectangle section at top	☐
4. **Apply base cream:** >> Entire hairline >> Tops of ears	☐

5. **Apply base cream to scalp:**
   - ¼" (.6 cm) to ½" (1.25 cm) horizontal partings
   - Use dabbing motion, without rubbing scalp

6. **Apply base cream to scalp using vertical partings:**
   - Repeat in same section using vertical partings

7. **Repeat base cream application to remaining sections:**
   - Use both horizontal and vertical partings

APPLY – AWAY FROM BASE THROUGH MIDSTRAND

8. **Begin relaxer application in back-right section:**
   - ¼" (.6 cm) horizontal partings
   - Apply ½" (1.25 cm) from the base through midstrand; not to ends
   - Apply to top and then bottom of each parting
   - Gently place hair up and out of the way

9. **Work to the bottom of section:**
   - When section is complete, gently bring lengths down

10. **Repeat technique on back-left section:**
    - Apply to top and then bottom of each parting
    - When section is complete, gently bring lengths down

| | ✔ |

11. Diagonal-back partings are used to apply relaxer to sides:

>> ¼" (.6 cm) diagonal-back partings

12. Apply relaxer to sides:

>> Apply ½" (1.25 cm) away from base through midstrand; not to ends
>> Bring lengths down when section complete

13. Repeat application on right side.

14. Apply relaxer to top section:

>> Horizontal partings
>> Apply to bottom of each parting, directing hair toward front

15. Apply to top of each parting:

>> Direct and position hair away from face
>> When section is complete, place lengths off to one side before proceeding

16. Apply relaxer to base and porous ends

>> Begin in back-right section
>> ¼" (.6 cm) horizontal partings
>> Apply relaxer to base; avoid direct contact with scalp
>> Then apply to porous ends
>> Place each parting up and out of the way as you work

17. Work downward using horizontal partings:

>> Bring lengths down when you complete section
>> Repeat on back-left section

18. Apply relaxer to sides:

>> ¼" (.6 cm) diagonal-back partings
>> Begin at top of section and work downward
>> Work from top to bottom of each section

19. Apply relaxer to top section:

>> Work from back to front
>> Apply to base and ends
>> Apply to bottom first then top
>> Keep hair out of face

20. Complete application by applying relaxer to entire hairline.

SMOOTH

21. Smooth back sections:

>> ¼" (.6 cm) horizontal partings
>> Use back of tail comb to smooth each parting
>> Smooth top of strand first, resting strand on palm of hand
>> Then smooth bottom of each parting, resting strand on palm
>> Direct parting upward
>> Work to bottom of section
>> Bring lengths down when complete

22. Smooth sides:

>> ¼" (.6 cm) diagonal-back partings
>> Smooth top then bottom of each parting
>> Bring lengths down when each section is complete

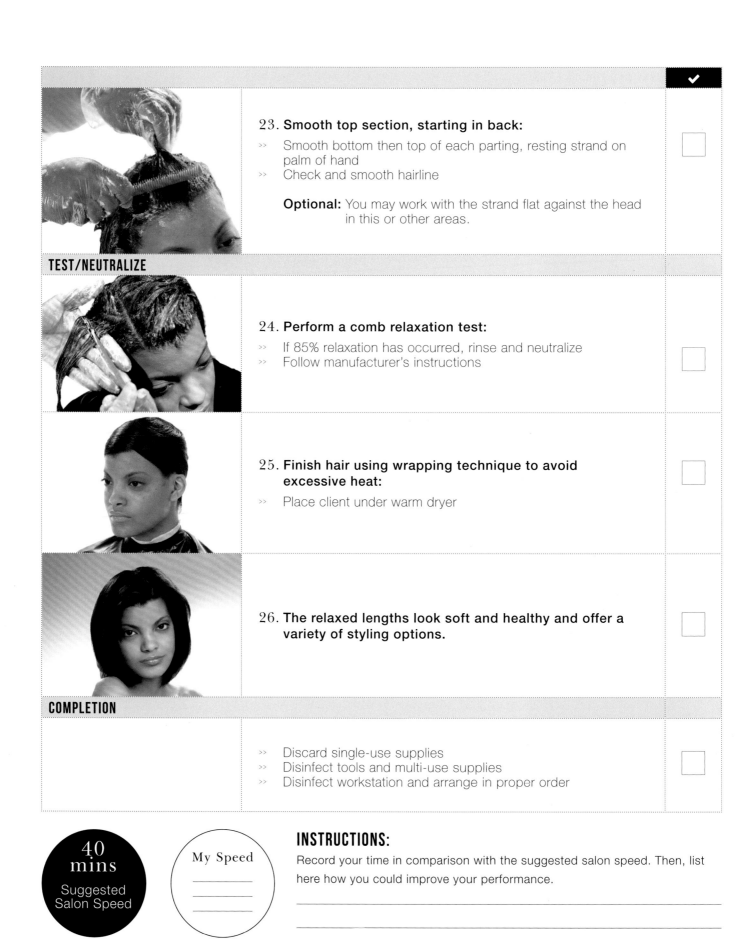

23. Smooth top section, starting in back:

>> Smooth bottom then top of each parting, resting strand on palm of hand
>> Check and smooth hairline

Optional: You may work with the strand flat against the head in this or other areas.

TEST/NEUTRALIZE

24. Perform a comb relaxation test:

>> If 85% relaxation has occurred, rinse and neutralize
>> Follow manufacturer's instructions

25. Finish hair using wrapping technique to avoid excessive heat:

>> Place client under warm dryer

26. The relaxed lengths look soft and healthy and offer a variety of styling options.

COMPLETION

>> Discard single-use supplies
>> Disinfect tools and multi-use supplies
>> Disinfect workstation and arrange in proper order

40 mins
Suggested Salon Speed

My Speed
_____
_____
_____

INSTRUCTIONS:

Record your time in comparison with the suggested salon speed. Then, list here how you could improve your performance.

_____

_____

_____

RETOUCH SODIUM HYDROXIDE RELAXER

EXPLORE

How do you think your expertise in performing a retouch sodium hydroxide relaxer could set you apart from other stylists?

INSPIRE

Your ability to perform the retouch sodium hydroxide relaxer service efficiently and accurately is important so your clients can rely on you to keep their hair in the very best condition.

ACHIEVE

Following this *Retouch Sodium Hydroxide Relaxer Workshop*, you'll be able to:

>> Identify the relaxer procedures related to the retouch sodium hydroxide relaxer

>> Relax new growth to create a repetition of smooth, straight texture, using consistent ¼" (.6 cm) horizontal and diagonal-back partings

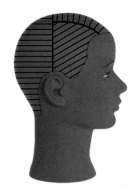

The finished relaxer design shows a correct amount of curl reduction, while maintaining the integrity and beauty of the hair. This workshop is performed on increase layers over a solid perimeter, with approximately 2.5" (6.25 cm) of new growth.

The head is sectioned into 5 sections. One-quarter inch (.6 cm) horizontal and diagonal-back partings are used to apply the relaxer product. One-half inch (1.25 cm) partings are used to apply protective cream to the previously relaxed hair. Relaxer is applied from the scalp up to the previously relaxed hair, being careful not to overlap.

RELAXER PROCEDURES

1. SECTION

2. APPLY

3. COMB OR SMOOTH

4. TEST

5 . NEUTRALIZE

DESIGN DECISIONS CHART

RETOUCH SODIUM HYDROXIDE RELAXER

Draw or fill in the boxes with the appropriate answers.

DESIGN DECISIONS

EXISTING TEXTURE

☐ ☐ ☐

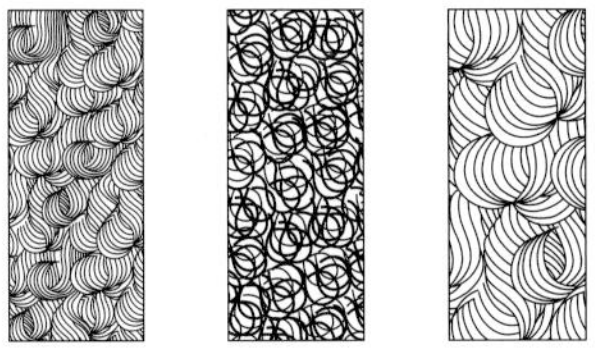

DESIRED TEXTURE

☐ ☐

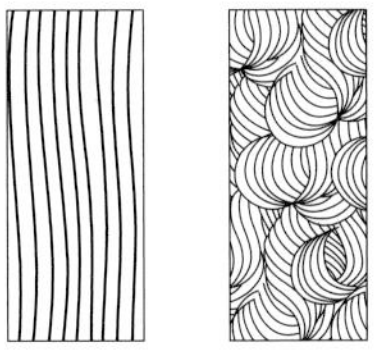

PRODUCT PLACEMENT

STRAND

☐ ☐

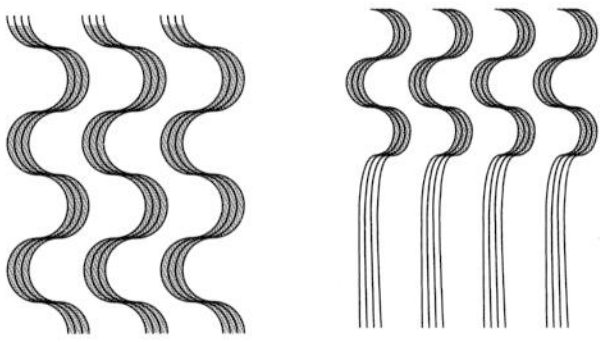

SECTIONING/PARTING PATTERN

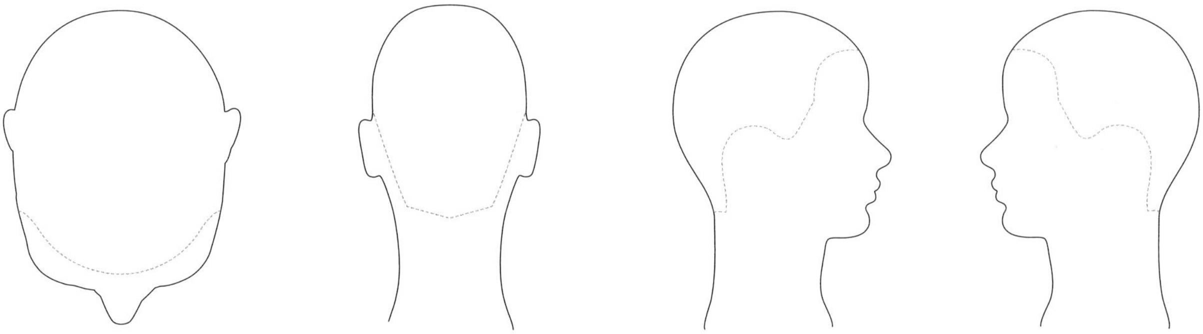

TOOL/PRODUCT CHOICE

____

____

____

Instructor Signature ______________________________ **Date** ________________

PERFORMANCE GUIDE

RETOUCH SODIUM HYDROXIDE RELAXER

View the video, complete the Design Decisions chart, then perform this workshop. Complete the self-check as you progress through the workshop.

30 mins
Suggested
Salon Speed

PREPARATION	✔
>> Assemble tools and products >> Set up workstation	☐

HAIR PREPARATION – HAIR AND SCALP ANALYSIS

1. **Perform scalp analysis.**

   Note: Hair must not be shampooed prior to the retouch sodium hydroxide relaxer service.

   ☐

SECTION/APPLY – BASE CREAM

2. **Apply base cream to:**
   - >> Entire hairline
   - >> Tops of ears
   - >> ¼" (.6 cm) horizontal partings throughout
   - >> Use dabbing motion to apply base without rubbing scalp

   ☐

3. **Apply base cream to:**
   - >> ¼" (.6 cm) vertical partings throughout

   ☐

APPLY PROTECTIVE CREAM

4. **Apply protective cream:**
   - >> Begin at back-right section
   - >> ½" (1.25 cm) horizontal partings
   - >> Apply from line of demarcation to ends
   - >> Apply to top and bottom of each parting
   - >> Repeat in remaining sections

   ☐

5. **Begin applying relaxer in back:**

   >> Outline back-right section, excluding nape hairline
   >> Start at the top of section
   >> ¼" (.6 cm) horizontal partings
   >> Apply relaxer to top and bottom of each parting, from scalp to previously relaxed hair
   >> Avoid overlapping onto previously relaxed hair
   >> Place hair up and out of way
   >> When section is complete, gently bring lengths down

6. **Repeat on back-left section.**

7. **Move to left side:**

   >> ¼" (.6 cm) diagonal-back partings
   >> Start at top of section

8. **Apply relaxer with same technique:**

   >> Outline section, excluding hairline
   >> Apply to top and bottom of each parting, only to new growth
   >> Bring lengths down when complete

9. **Repeat the same techniques on the right side.**

10. **Apply relaxer to top section:**

    >> Start at back of section
    >> Outline section, excluding hairline
    >> Apply to bottom and then top of each parting
    >> Direct and position hair away from face
    >> When completed, place lengths off to one side before proceeding

11. **Apply relaxer to entire hairline.**

SMOOTH ✔

12. Smooth back sections:

>> Outline back-right section, using back of tail comb to smooth new growth area against head
>> Use back of tail comb to smooth each parting against head
>> ¼" (.6 cm) horizontal partings
>> Smooth top, then bottom of each parting
>> Direct partings upward
>> Work to bottom of section
>> Bring lengths down when completed
>> Repeat on back-left side

13. Smooth sides:

>> ¼" (.6 cm) diagonal-back partings
>> Start at top of left side
>> Smooth top and bottom of each parting
>> Bring lengths down when section is complete
>> Repeat on right side

14. Smooth top section:

>> Work from back to front
>> Direct hair away from face
>> Check and smooth entire hairline

TEST/NEUTRALIZE

15. Perform a comb relaxation test:

>> If 85% relaxation has occurred, rinse and neutralize
>> Follow manufacturer's instructions

FINISH

16. Air form hair for a smooth finish:

>> Place client under warm hood dryer or use blow dryer with low heat to remove 85% of moisture
>> Then use horizontal partings and a 9-row brush to air form

17. **Finish smoothing hair with warm flat iron:**
    >> Begin in nape, using horizontal partings
    >> Use tail of comb to lift hair into desired base position
    >> Place flat iron at base and move toward ends in curved motion
    >> Work to top of back section

18. **Smooth sides using same technique:**
    >> Work from bottom to top of one side
    >> Repeat on the opposite side

    Note: In this design, a side part is used.

19. **The finished relaxer retouch displays the correct amount of curl reduction throughout, while maintaining the integrity and beauty of the hair.**

COMPLETION

>> Discard single-use supplies
>> Disinfect tools and multi-use supplies
>> Disinfect workstation and arrange in proper order

30 mins
Suggested
Salon Speed

My Speed
_____
_____
_____

INSTRUCTIONS:
Record your time in comparison with the suggested salon speed. Then, list here how you could improve your performance.

_____
_____
_____
_____
_____

CURL REFORMATION THEORY | 111ᶜ.20

EXPLORE //

Do you know someone with tightly curled hair texture who has tried several products in hopes of attaining a more defined curl or wave pattern?

INSPIRE //

With a knowledge and understanding of curl reformation services, you can offer options to your clients with tightly curled hair beyond relaxer services.

ACHIEVE //

Following this lesson on *Curl Reformation Theory*, you'll be able to:

>> State the milestones that influenced curl reformation services as we know them today

>> Explain the two processes involved in performing a curl reformation service

>> Provide examples of products, supplies and equipment used to perform a curl reformation service

>> Identify and explain the six procedural steps during the curl reformation service

>> Describe the three areas of a curl reformation service

FOCUS //

CURL REFORMATION THEORY	
History of Curl Reforming	Curl Reformation Skills
Curl Reforming Processes	Curl Reformation Guest Experience
Curl Reformation Products and Essentials	Curl Reformation Service
	Curl Reformation Rubric

Clients with tightly curled hair might prefer the look and feel of looser curls. You can offer these clients a curl reformation service, which reforms tightly curled hair into more defined curls and waves.

Curl reformation is a chemical service designed to change tightly curled hair to curly or wavy hair. Curl reformation is also known as soft curls, reformation curls or double-process perm. The hair is first relaxed to reduce the natural curl pattern and then permed to create a new curl pattern.

Actions in the curl reformation process include:

» **Reduce** the existing curl pattern

» **Reform** to produce a new curl pattern around perm tools

» **Rebond** to fix (neutralize) the chemical bonds and lock in the new curl pattern

Note that much of the information you have already learned about perming and relaxing hair will apply to curl reformation services. In this lesson, we will primarily highlight the critical areas that are different when performing curl reformation services.

CURL REFORMATION THEORY

HISTORY OF CURL REFORMING

The curl reformation service was intended to provide a more defined curl pattern for people with tightly curled hair and an easier method to style and maintain their hair. At the time, relaxers were the only option for straightening the natural curl pattern, and many clients experienced dry, brittle hair and breakage.

As with many innovations in the hair industry, it can be difficult to pinpoint exactly who made discoveries. However, we can certainly look at leaders and innovators who affected change in the industry. Such is the case with curl reformation.

In the 1970s, Dr. Willie Morrow started a company called California Curl, in which he created a cold wave formulated to produce soft curls for tightly curled hair.

During this time, Jheri Redding, co-founder of Redken, Jhirmack and Nexxus® (also credited for the creation of pH-balanced shampoo) developed the "Jheri curl" which was also a cold wave reforming system formulated for tightly curled hair. The Jheri curl—worn by men and women alike—was popular among African-Americans, especially famous entertainers and athletes.

The Jheri curl was promoted as a low-maintenance, wash-and-wear style that was easier to take care of than a chemical relaxer. However, the daily maintenance product, curl activator, contained oils that could stain clothing and pillows.

In 1980, Comer Cottrell, the founder of Pro-Line hair care products company created the first at-home system called Pro-Line's Curly Kit. The Jheri Curl could be expensive and was only available in professional salons, but people could use a "curly kit" to obtain similar results at home. The curly kits were so popular that in their first year, Pro-Line's sales grew from $1 million to more than $10 million. In 1981, *Forbes* magazine called the curly kit the biggest single product ever to hit the African-American cosmetics market.

By the late 1980s the reformation curl had started to diminish in popularity and relaxers became more popular. Many manufacturers attempted to create systems that were intended to transition clients from a curl reformation to a chemical relaxer. Since most relaxers were hydroxide-based, many of these products were unsuccessful.

Today, curl reformation products have been reformulated and are often known as "dry-curl systems." These systems produce beautiful soft curls without the wet, oily look of earlier systems. Many dry-curl systems also offer more styling versatility, giving clients the option to straighten the hair with heat as well.

BASIC CURL REFORMATION SERVICES

There are two basic curl reformation services: virgin curl reformation and retouch curl reformation.

» **A virgin curl reformation** service is used on natural, untreated or "virgin" hair to reform tightly curled texture into a looser curl or wave pattern.

» **A retouch curl reformation** service is performed on the new growth only to match the previously curl reformed hair.

CURL REFORMING PROCESSES

You've learned in previous lessons how to perm the hair and relax the hair. The curl reformation service creates a new, looser curl pattern by utilizing both processes: first relaxing, then perming.

1. The first process involves relaxing or **reducing** the natural curl pattern by:

» Applying a thio-based product known as a curl rearranger

» Smoothing the hair to relax or **reduce** natural curl pattern

2. The second process involves perming or **reforming** and **rebonding** the hair into a new curl or wave pattern.

» Wrap and secure the hair using perm tools to **reform** hair to new curl or wave pattern.

» Any perm wrapping pattern can be used to wrap the hair once the desired direction is established.

» Generally, 1 diameter (1x) half-off base control is used throughout.

» Apply curl booster, which is a creamy thio-based lotion, to the hair.

» Curl booster may be applied before and/or after wrapping, depending on manufacturer's directions and the designer's speed and skill.

» Rinse and apply neutralizer to **rebond** hair into new curl or wave pattern.

CURL REFORMATION PRODUCTS AND ESSENTIALS

To perform professional curl reformation services, you need a selection of products, tools/rods, supplies and equipment. Most of these will be familiar to you from your studies in perming and relaxing. Here, we will highlight those products, tools and essentials that are specific to curl reformation services.

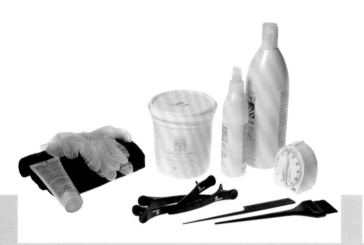

PRODUCTS

While a curl reformation service may include steps and products that are similar to those used in perm and relaxer services, it is important that you use products specifically formulated for curl reformations and follow manufacturer's directions carefully.

Curl Rearranger

In the **reducing** step, a curl rearranger (reducing product) is applied to the hair. **The curl rearranger is the product used to reduce or relax the natural curl pattern.** The application procedures are the same as in chemical relaxing. The following are points to know about curl rearrangers:

>> **Ammonium thioglycolate is the main ingredient found in curl rearrangers.**

>> Thio is an alkaline chemical available in cream, lotion or gel.

>> It is called a curl rearranger because it shifts and rearranges the polypeptide chains and disulfide bonds of the hair, the same as in perming.

>> It is available in mild for fine hair, regular for average hair, and super for resistant hair.

>> Since the descriptions of strengths may vary among manufacturers, be sure to read the manufacturer's directions carefully.

Curl Booster and Perm Solution

In the **reforming** step, a curl booster, or perm solution, is applied to the hair:

>> Mild, creamy form of ammonium thioglycolate is the main ingredient

>> Causes hair to soften and swell in order to be reformed into curl or wave pattern

>> Can be applied before or after wrapping hair on perm rods

   ▪ If wrapped with booster, more booster is usually applied after wrapping is complete to ensure thorough saturation

Neutralizer

Once the test curl displays the desired curl formation, the hair is rinsed and a neutralizing (bonding) lotion is applied to reform (fix) the curl into a lasting shape.

The neutralizer:

>> Locks in the new curl pattern that was created in the reforming step

>> Reduces swelling caused by alkaline formulas

>> Causes oxidation, which restores broken down disulfide bonds

>> Results in hair being held in new curl pattern

>> Is applied to perm tools and remains in the hair for the full recommended processing time

   ▪ Neutralizing with perm rods in the hair will result in a firmer curl pattern

   ▪ For a looser pattern, apply neutralizer to perm rods then remove the rods and apply additional neutralizer for the remaining processing time

Be careful during this service to ensure satisfactory results. **Extended processing time, combined with dual application of processing solutions can damage the hair.** Follow manufacturer's directions closely.

DISCOVER**MORE**

Take the time to research new products, developments and education in the curl reformation market. Curl reformation services are evolving with advancements in formulations and products to protect the hair and keep it in the best possible condition. These advancements help you provide exceptional curl reformation services, giving your clients more styling options.

Employers are required to make Safety Data Sheets (SDS) for all products available for your reference and use in the salon.

Curl reforming products are produced by many different manufacturers, are disposable, and must be frequently replaced.

Curl Reformation Products

The following chart highlights the products that are specific to curl reformation services. Other products that may be used in a curl reformation service can be found in the *Relaxer Products and Essentials* lesson.

PRODUCTS	FUNCTION
Curl Rearranger	Reduces peptide bonds so hair can relax; thio-based product
Curl Booster	Helps hair assume new shape of perm tool; milder form of thio
Curl Activator	Helps new curl configurations retain their shape and provides moisture; applied frequently after every shampoo
Instant Moisturizer	Helps replace natural moisture and oils lost during chemical processes

ESSENTIALS

Curl reformation tools are the hand-held tools you use to provide a professional service. In addition to the applicator brush, non-metal tail comb and shampoo comb used in relaxer services (see the *Relaxer Products and Essentials* lesson), you will need:

» Perm rods

    ▪ Determine shape and size of new curl
    ▪ Selected by shape, diameter and length

To perform curl reformation services in the salon, you need various supplies and equipment. These are mostly the same as used in relaxer services (see the *Relaxer Products and Essentials* lesson).

Curl Reformation Supplies

The supplies include a protective shampoo cape, cloth towels, a neutralizing bib or cape, a bowl, a protective smock or apron, spatula(s), protective gloves, plastic sectioning clips, a plastic bag or cap and the Chemical Service record.
You will also need:

» Stabilizers or picks – Hold perm tools in position when placed under the perm tool band

» End papers – Control the hair ends when wrapping

Curl Reformation Equipment

Just like a relaxer service, the equipment you need to perform a curl reformation service includes a hood dryer, a timer, shampoo bowl and styling chair. See the *Relaxer Products and Essentials* lesson.

Understanding the different relaxer product and tool choices available allows you to make your selection based on the desired end result and your client's hair type, while maintaining the integrity of the hair.

CURL REFORMATION SKILLS

Careful analysis of your client's hair and your ability to apply the necessary skills will allow you to create beautiful curl reformation designs for your clients.

PRE-CURL REFORMATION ANALYSIS

Before beginning any chemical service, you will perform a hair analysis to properly assess the condition of your client's hair. The porosity, elasticity, texture, density, type of curl pattern and overall condition of the hair will help determine the appropriate type of service you'll provide and the type and strength of curl reformation products to use. See the *Perm Skills* and *Relaxer Skills* lessons for more information about appropriate hair analysis for a curl reformation service. Just as with perming and relaxing, a complete and thorough analysis should be performed before a curl reformation service.

CURL REFORMATION STEPS

The client who requests a curl reformation service is usually sure that this is the service they really want. However, if this client's hair has been previously relaxed, you will need to make sure that the relaxer product used was an ammonium thioglycolate-based product. Hair that has been treated with a sodium hydroxide-based relaxer cannot receive this service since the two chemicals are not compatible.

The steps that are performed within a curl reformation service are:

1. Section

2. Apply curl rearranger

3. Smooth

4. Section and wrap

5. Apply curl booster

6. Neutralize

ECTION

The hair is sectioned to organize and control the lengths during the application.

For the application of the curl rearranger, the hair can be sectioned into four or five sections, just like in a relaxer service.

PPLY CURL REARRANGER

This part of the curl reformation service is performed with an ammonium thioglycolate-based product as described in the *Relaxer Skills* lesson.

In a virgin application, the rearranger is applied to the midstrand or cold shaft first, and then to the base and the ends

In a retouch application, the rearranger is only applied to the new-growth area without overlapping onto hair that has been previously treated.

An applicator brush is recommended to apply product, usually to both sides of the hairstrand to ensure even distribution and penetration. Wear protective gloves while working with the chemicals involved in a curl reformation service.

MOOTH

The back of a comb is used to smooth the hair for this portion of the curl reformation service, just as in a relaxer service. A virgin application is smoothed from base to ends. Only the new growth is smoothed in a retouch application, with special care taken not to overlap product onto previously treated hair.

Note that the hair will be thoroughly rinsed but not neutralized prior to the next step.

ECTION AND WRAP

Since the hair will now be wrapped to create a new curl formation, the hair must be sectioned according to the desired wrapping pattern. Curl reformation services are usually performed on short-to-medium lengths. The same wrapping patterns seen in the *Perm Design* lesson are applicable to curl reformation services.

Sectioning will be based on the wrapping pattern that you choose to work with. Since the curl has just been reduced, remember that the hair is in a fragile state and must be treated gently.

Regardless of the wrapping pattern used with rods:
>> 1x bases are generally used with half-of base control
>> Picks or stabilizers can be positioned as needed
>> Tool position and stability should be checked before proceeding to the next application step

PPLY CURL BOOSTER

The next step of the curl reformation service is the application of curl booster. To ensure saturation, the curl booster is applied to the top and bottom of each rod after wrapping the hair in the desired pattern.

Well-experienced designers sometimes choose to apply the curl booster section by section prior to wrapping. This method requires great manual dexterity in order to wrap the hair quickly enough. It is best to follow the manufacturer's instructions for processing and rinsing the curl booster.

EUTRALIZE

Generally, neutralizing is done while the hair is still wrapped on the perm rods. The process is very similar to neutralizing a perm. Again, it is best to follow the manufacturer's instructions for timing and rinsing of the neutralizer.

When performing a curl reformation service, the perm tool diameter chosen is generally at least two times larger than the diameter of the natural curl pattern. Since this service results in some natural texture remaining in the hair, thinner partings are used while wrapping.

CURL REFORMATION GUEST EXPERIENCE

Before applying any curl reforming chemicals to the hair, have a thorough consultation with the client. Listen carefully and record all the important information in the client's chemical records. Be sure you understand the new texture pattern your client desires. Ask questions to determine past and current products used on the hair. Follow the same service essentials you learned in the *Relaxer Guest Experience* lesson.

COMMUNICATION GUIDELINES

You'll need to advise your curl reformation clients regarding the services that can effectively be added to a curl reformation service to achieve the looks they want. You and your client will determine if a hair sculpture or color service is compatible with the curl reformation service. These guidelines will help you communicate with your clients as you explore available options.

COMBINATION SERVICES

>> Hair sculpting is usually performed after the curl reformation service to modify the existing sculpture or to create a completely new design. Working with the new curl or wave pattern may require adjustments to the sculpted form. If a significant amount of length is to be removed, you may choose to sculpt the hair prior to the curl reformation service.

>> Avoid coloring the hair immediately after a curl reformation service to prevent color fading and adverse results. A period of 7-14 days is recommended after the curl reformation service before coloring the hair with permanent color, including highlights. Since the hair has already received multiple chemical processes in the curl reformation service, it is not recommend to perform color services that require lightener (bleach).

It is also essential that you help your curl reformation clients care for their hair at home. The following guidelines may help you determine what additional services to offer these clients as well as how to approach their at-home care practices to set up a successful maintenance regimen.

AT-HOME CARE AND PRODUCTS

>> Shampooing should be performed every 1½ -2 weeks. Clients should be advised that freshly shampooed hair usually takes one or two days to regain its ideal moisture balance.

>> Clients who receive a curl reformation service must be made aware of the necessity for moisturizing products in their home hair care regimen. These products are usually applied to towel-dried hair and combed through with a wide-tooth comb. Manufacturers may recommend specific products that are especially beneficial.

>> A blow dryer set on medium or low heat can be used with a diffuser, or the client may sit beneath a hood dryer to dry the hair. Air drying may also be an option. Whichever method is used, it is important not to overdry the hair.

>> It is often recommended that the curl reformation client return to the salon one week after the service to receive the first shampoo and conditioner. This allows the designer to assess the condition of the hair and make any necessary recommendations.

>> Advise curl reformation clients to use the manufacturer's maintenance products to shampoo and condition the hair, following the manufacturer's instructions. This includes the use of deep conditioning treatments.

CURL REFORMATION INFECTION CONTROL AND SAFETY

Always adhere to proper safety precautions prior to and during a curl reformation service to protect the client and yourself. Below are points specific to the curl reformation service. See the *Perm Guest Experience* and *Relaxer Guest Experience* lessons for more infection control and safety information.

1. Shampoo the client's hair only once prior to a curl reformation service to avoid sensitizing the scalp. Use light finger pressure and moderate water pressure with a mild temperature.

2. Never perform a curl reformation service on hair that has been relaxed with a sodium hydroxide relaxer. This can result in severe breakage and/or irreversible damage.

Refer to the *Perm Guest Experience* and *Relaxer Guest Experience* lessons for information on the following:

Draping for Chemical Services

Scalp Analysis

Test for Metallic Salts

PRELIMINARY STRAND TEST

Preliminary strand testing is a good predictor of how your client's hair will react to the curl rearranger, booster and neutralizer. Always take the time to test tinted, bleached, overporous or damaged hair.

>> Shampoo and towel-dry hair.
>> Apply base cream on scalp and hairline.
>> Follow manufacturer's directions and test the most delicate areas of the hair. Wrap a coil of cotton around strand to isolate it from the rest of the hair.
>> Apply curl rearranger to the hair, then smooth, rinse and blot it.
>> Apply the booster and wrap the strand on a perm rod.
>> Set a timer and process according to manufacturer's directions.
>> Pay close attention and check the hair frequently.
>> Unfasten and carefully unwind the hair about 1½-2 turns of the rod to check the test curl. Do not permit the hair to loosen or unwind from the perm rod completely. Hold the hair firmly by placing a thumb at each end of the rod. Turn it gently toward the scalp so that the hair falls easily into the wave pattern. Do not push the perm rod toward the head. Continue checking until a firm curl pattern forms, equal to the rod's diameter.
>> Process, rinse and neutralize the test strand.
>> Evaluate and document the results.

CLEANING AND DISINFECTION GUIDELINES

Follow the same cleaning and disinfection guidelines found in the *Perm Guest Experience* and *Relaxer Guest Experience* lessons.

CARE AND SAFETY

Follow the same infection control procedures for personal care and client safety guidelines before and during the curl reformation service that you would for a perm or relaxer service to ensure your safety and the client's, while also contributing to the salon care. These precautions will protect you and the client and ensure a safe work environment. See the *Perm Guest Experience* and *Relaxer Guest Experience* lessons for specific information.

 Alert! If tools, multi-use supplies or equipment have come in contact with blood or body fluids, the following disinfection procedures must take place: **Use an approved EPA-registered hospital disinfectant according to manufacturer's directions and as required by your area's regulatory agency.**

CURL REFORMATION SERVICE

The following curl reformation service procedures incorporate what you have learned about curl reformation theory, tools, skills and guest relations. Applying this knowledge will ensure client safety and satisfaction.

Client-centered guidelines help develop your chair-side manner. This builds trust and loyalty among your clients and leads to career success for you.

PROCEDURAL GUIDELINES

The procedural guidelines that will help you ensure your client's comfort and safety during the curl reformation service are the same guidelines that you would use to perform perm and relaxer services. The relaxer guidelines pertain to the first three steps: section, apply curl rearranger and smooth. The perm guidelines are more applicable for the last three steps: section and wrap, apply curl booster and neutralize. See the *Perm Service* and the *Relaxer Service* lessons for details on these guidelines.

Check with your regulatory agency for proper application procedures to use while you are in school.

Service Essentials: The Four Cs

The hair design procedures include attention to the Four Cs.

1. **Connect**
   Establishes rapport and builds credibility with each client

2. **Consult**
   Analyzes client wants and needs, visualizes the end result, organizes the plan for follow-through and obtains client agreement

3. **Create**
   Produces functional, predictable and pleasing results

4. **Complete**
   Reviews the service experience and client satisfaction, offers product recommendations, expresses appreciation and provides follow-up

CURL REFORMATION SERVICE OVERVIEW

The Curl Reformation Service Overview identifies the three areas of all curl reformation services:

>> Curl Reformation Preparation provides a brief overview of the steps to follow *before* you actually begin the curl reformation service.

>> Curl Reformation Procedure provides an overview of the procedures you will use *during* the curl reformation service to ensure predictable results.

>> Curl Reformation Completion provides an overview of the steps to follow *after* performing the curl reformation service to ensure guest satisfaction.

CURL REFORMATION SERVICE OVERVIEW

CURL REFORMATION PREPARATION	» Clean and disinfect workstation. » Assemble curl reformation essentials including sectioning clips, non-metal tail comb, gloves, base cream, relaxer, bowl, applicator brush, perm rods, picks/stabilizers and end papers. » Wash hands. » Perform analysis of hair and scalp. » Ask client to remove jewelry; store in a secure place. » Perform preliminary strand test and elasticity test. » Review previous client record if applicable.

CURL REFORMATION PROCEDURE	» Drape client for the service.
	» Pre-shampoo the hair lightly.
	» **Section** hair into 5 sections.
	» Apply base cream around hairline and tops of ears.
	» **Apply** and **smooth** hair with curl rearranger following the same procedures for a virgin relaxer application, except for neutralizing.
	» Follow manufacturer's directions for processing.
	» Rinse thoroughly and towel-blot hair; *do not neutralize*.
	» Distribute the hair in the direction the hair will be worn.
	» Section hair according to the desired wrapping pattern.
	» **Wrap** using a 1x half-off base control or other base control, depending on desired result.
	» Secure perm rods with stabilizers or picks.
	» Apply barrier cream and position cotton along hairline.
	» **Apply** curl booster; process according to manufacturer's directions.
	» Take test curls, if needed.
	» Rinse curl booster and towel-blot each rod.
	» **Neutralize** according to the manufacturer's directions.
	  ▪ Apply neutralizer.
	  ▪ Remove perm tools and rinse neutralizer.
	» Finish curl reformation design.

CURL REFORMATION COMPLETION	» Reinforce client's satisfaction with overall salon experience. » Make professional product recommendations. » Prebook client's next appointment. » End client's visit with warm and personal goodbye. » Discard single-use supplies; disinfect tools and multi-use supplies; disinfect workstation and arrange in proper order. » Wash your hands. » Complete client record.

Problems you may encounter in a curl reformation service are generally the same as those you would encounter in a perm and/or relaxer service. Refer to the *Perm Service* and *Relaxer Service* lessons to review some of the problems you could encounter and possible solutions.

CURL REFORMATION RUBRIC

A performance rubric is a document that identifies criteria at which levels of performance can be measured objectively. The following rubric is an example that your instructor might choose to use for scoring. The Curl Reformation Rubric is divided into three main areas—Preparation, Procedure and Completion. Each area is further divided into step-by-step procedures that will ensure client safety and satisfaction.

CURL REFORMATION RUBRIC

Allotted Time: 1 hour, 30 Minutes

Student Name: _____ ID Number: _____

Instructor: _____ Date: _____ Start Time: _____ End Time: _____

CURL REFORMATION (Live Model) – Each scoring item is marked with either a "Yes" or "No." Each "Yes" counts for one point. Total number of points attainable is 37.

CRITERIA	YES	NO	INSTRUCTOR ASSESSMENT
PREPARATION: *Did student...*			
1. Set up workstation with properly labeled supplies?	☐	☐	
2. Place disinfected tools and supplies at a visibly clean workstation?	☐	☐	
3. Wash hands?	☐	☐	
Connect: Did student...			
4. Meet and greet client with a welcoming smile and pleasant tone of voice?	☐	☐	
5. Communicate to build rapport and develop a relationship with client?	☐	☐	
6. Refer to client by name throughout service?	☐	☐	
Consult: Did student...			
7. Ask questions to discover client's wants and needs?	☐	☐	
8. Analyze client's hair and scalp and check for any contraindications?	☐	☐	
9. Gain feedback and consent from client before proceeding?	☐	☐	
PROCEDURE: *Did student...*			
10. Properly drape client and prepare for service?	☐	☐	
11. Ensure client protection and comfort by maintaining cape on outside of chair at all times?	☐	☐	
12. Carry out appropriate shampoo and condition procedures when applicable?	☐	☐	
13. Use products and supplies economically?	☐	☐	
Create: Did student...			
14. Follow the procedure for a virgin thio relaxer, prior to neutralizing?	☐	☐	
15. Distribute and section hair appropriately for curl reformation pattern?	☐	☐	
16. Use correct wrapping techniques to include partings, end papers and base controls?	☐	☐	
17. Use correct securing technique?	☐	☐	
18. Prepare curl reformation products correctly?	☐	☐	
19. Apply barrier cream and cotton strip properly to protect skin?	☐	☐	
20. Apply curl booster accurately to each rod, saturating hair?	☐	☐	
21. Apply plastic cap and/or heat according to manufacturer's directions?	☐	☐	
22. Process curl booster according to manufacturer's directions?	☐	☐	
23. Perform test curl to ensure proper curl development?	☐	☐	
24. Rinse thoroughly to remove curl booster from hair and towel-blot hair?	☐	☐	
25. Apply and process neutralizer according to manufacturer's directions?	☐	☐	
26. Rinse thoroughly to remove neutralizer from hair and towel-blot hair?	☐	☐	
27. Teach client to use products to maintain appearance and condition of hair?	☐	☐	
28. Practice infection control procedures and safety guidelines throughout service?	☐	☐	
COMPLETION (*Complete*): *Did student...*			
29. Ask questions and look for verbal and nonverbal cues to determine client's level of satisfaction?	☐	☐	
30. Make professional product recommendations?	☐	☐	
31. Ask client to make a future appointment?	☐	☐	
32. End client's visit with a warm and personal goodbye?	☐	☐	
33. Discard single-use supplies?	☐	☐	
34. Disinfect tools and multi-use supplies; disinfect workstation and arrange in proper order?	☐	☐	
35. Complete service within scheduled time?	☐	☐	
36. Complete client record?	☐	☐	
37. Wash their hands following service?	☐	☐	

COMMENTS: _____ TOTAL POINTS = _____ ÷ 37 = _____ %

Knowledge of curl reformation services will enable you to offer these services to clients with tightly curled hair so they can enjoy more defined curls and waves.

LESSONS LEARNED

>> The first curl reforming product was created in the 1970s to provide people with tightly curled hair an easier method of styling and maintaining their hair. Among the first were Pro-Line products, California Curl and a system that became known as the Jheri curl.

>> The curl reformation service creates a new, looser curl pattern by utilizing two processes:

■ The first process involves relaxing or reducing the natural curl pattern.

■ The second process involves perming or reforming and rebonding the hair into a new curl or wave pattern.

>> The curl reformation service uses similar products, supplies and equipment as the perm and relaxer services, such as rods, picks/stabilizers, end papers and neutralizer. Additional products used in curl reformation include curl booster, curl rearranger, curl activator and instant moisturizer.

>> The procedural steps in a curl reformation service include:

■ Section hair to allow better control of the lengths during application.

■ Apply curl rearranger to the midstrand, then base and ends.

■ Smooth hair with the back of the comb, as in a relaxer service.

■ Section and wrap the hair to create the new curl formation.

■ Apply curl booster to the top and bottom of each rod to ensure saturation.

■ Neutralize the hair to lock in the new curl pattern.

>> The three areas of a curl reformation service include the Preparation, Procedure and Completion:

■ Preparation includes greeting the client, arranging workstation and performing a hair and scalp analysis.

■ Procedure includes following the curl reformation steps to properly reduce and reform the desired curl pattern.

■ Completion includes reinforcing client's satisfaction, making product recommendations, prebooking next appointment and disinfecting workstation.

VIRGIN CURL REFORMATION

EXPLORE

What cues or statements from a client might lead you to recommend a curl reformation service?

INSPIRE

This service is perfect for clients who want more defined and manageable curls and helps you create a desired texture, while maintaining the integrity of the hair.

ACHIEVE

Following this *Virgin Curl Reformation Workshop*, you'll be able to:

>> Identify the relaxer procedures related to the virgin curl reformation

>> Identify the appropriate length rods to adapt to the width of each shape in the contour perm pattern

>> Create a repetition of curl on uniformly layered lengths using 1x, half-off base control throughout

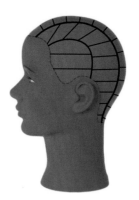

A repetition of curl texture on uniformly layered lengths moves away from the face through the center and downward at the sides.

The contour pattern used for this curl reformation positions a center rectangle from the front hairline to the nape, which becomes slightly narrower in the nape. Sections on either side follow the contours of the head, and the sides are wrapped horizontally. The hair is wrapped to move primarily away from the face.

CURL REFORMATION PROCEDURES

1. SECTION

2. APPLY CURL REARRANGER

3. SMOOTH

4. SECTION AND WRAP

5. APPLY CURL BOOSTER

6. NEUTRALIZE

DESIGN DECISIONS CHART

VIRGIN CURL REFORMATION

Draw or fill in the boxes with the appropriate answers.

DESIGN DECISIONS

EXISTING TEXTURE

☐ ☐ ☐

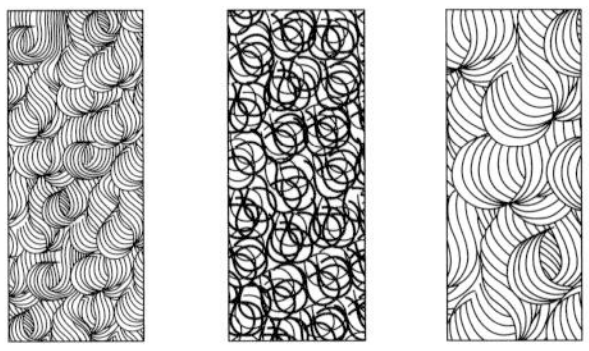

DESIRED TEXTURE

☐ ☐ ☐ ☐

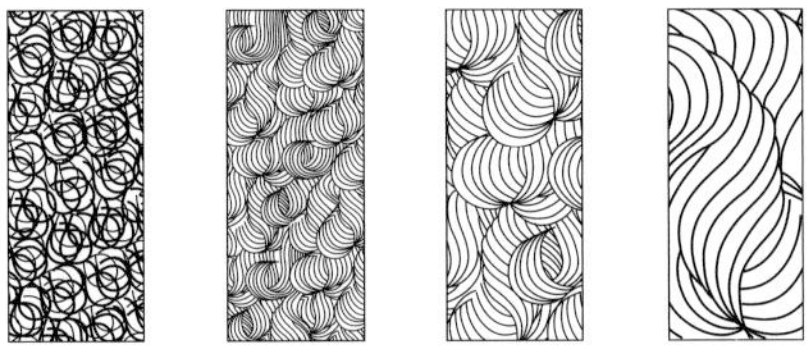

TEXTURE PLACEMENT

STRAND

☐ ☐

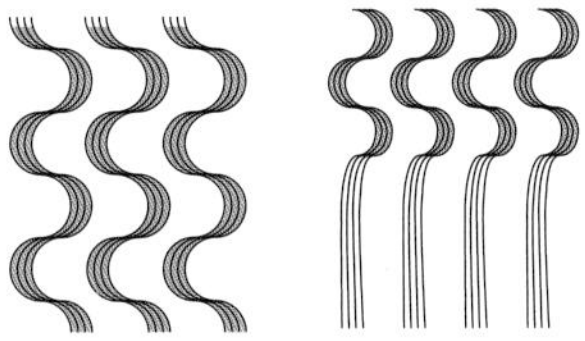

DESIGN PRINCIPLES

☐ ☐ ☐ ☐

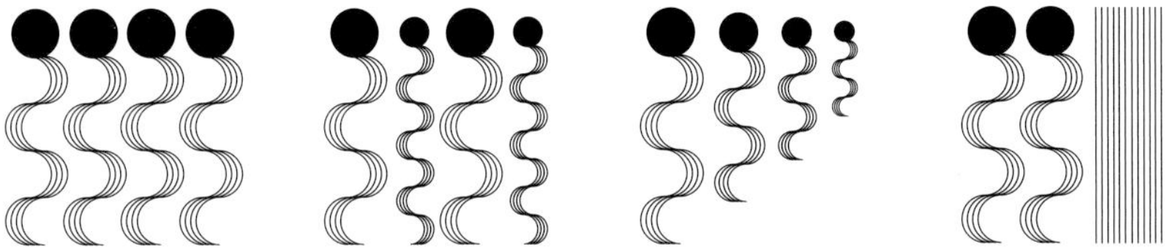

TOOL DIAMETER CHOICES

☐ ☐ ☐

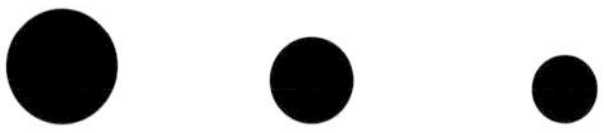

WRAPPING PATTERN/DIRECTION

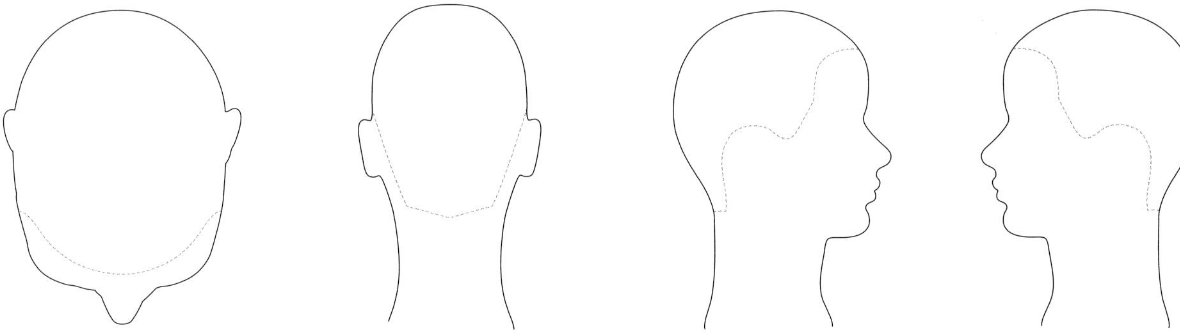

TOOL/PRODUCT CHOICE

____

____

____

Instructor Signature ____________________________ **Date** ______________

PERFORMANCE GUIDE
VIRGIN CURL REFORMATION

View the video, complete the Design Decisions chart, then perform this workshop. Complete the self-check as you progress through the workshop.

2 hrs
Suggested
Salon Speed

PREPARATION ✔

>> Assemble tools and products
>> Set up workstation
>> Shampoo hair

Note: Do not condition.

☐

SECTION/APPLY CURL REARRANGER/SMOOTH – ENTIRE HEAD

1. **Perform procedure for a virgin thio relaxer service, excluding neutralizer.**

   Note: Do not neutralize.

☐

SECTION/CONTOUR PATTERN, WRAP, CENTER RECTANGLE

2. **Section center rectangle:**
   >> Distribute hair back off the face
   >> Start at hairline
   >> Use length of rod to determine width of rectangle
   >> Use tail comb to section

☐

3. **Measure and section back of rectangle:**
   >> Use shorter tool to adapt shape to be narrower in nape

☐

4. **Begin wrapping at front hairline:**
   - 1x horizontal base
   - 90° projection
   - Bookend end-paper technique
   - Overlap wrapping technique
   - Position rod half-off base
   - Fasten band across rod
   - Position pick or stabilizer temporarily toward face

5. **Wrap center rectangle through crown:**
   - Maintain 90° from center of each base to achieve half-off base control
   - Maintain consistent tension
   - Secure with stabilizers or picks in direction of wrap

6. **Wrap center rectangle through nape with shorter rods to adapt as the rectangle narrows in nape:**
   - Switch to shorter rods used to measure
   - Wrap and secure with same technique

SECTION/WRAP – SIDE

7. **Measure and section next to center rectangle:**
   - Diagonal-forward partings at front hairline
   - Length of rod to determine width
   - Indirect partings from multiple points of origin
   - Partings gradually become horizontal partings through nape

8. Begin wrapping at front hairline with diagonal-forward partings and the same wrapping technique.

9. Continue working toward back of shape:
   >> Take partings and position rods to follow curve of head

10. Change to horizontal partings and rod positions as you work toward the nape:
    >> Adapt length of rod to size of section
    >> Position stabilizers or picks to secure

11. Wrap remaining shape:
    >> Horizontal partings
    >> Overlap technique
    >> Half-off base control
    >> Adapt rod length to accommodate hairline

12. Repeat same sectioning and wrapping techniques on opposite side.

APPLY CURL BOOSTER/NEUTRALIZE

13. Place cotton around hairline and saturate hair with curl booster:
   >> Process and neutralize according to manufacturer's directions

14. The finished curl reformation contains soft, manageable curls, with a repetition of curl diameter for greater style versatility.

COMPLETION

>> Discard single-use supplies
>> Disinfect tools and multi-use supplies
>> Disinfect workstation and arrange in proper order

2 hrs
Suggested Salon Speed

My Speed
_____
_____
_____

INSTRUCTIONS:
Record your time in comparison with the suggested salon speed. Then, list here how you could improve your performance.

_____
_____
_____
_____

» 111^c GLOSSARY/INDEX

Cushion Technique   *54*
End paper wrapping technique that incorporates several end papers; cushions and supports fragile hair and controls shorter lengths within the hair section.

Density   *45, 145*
Describes the amount of hair follicles per square inch on the scalp and is usually referred to as light, medium or heavy (thin, medium or thick). Hair density does not always correspond to hair texture.

Design Decisions   *16*
Process of making choices between design alternatives based on client communication and anatomy, as well as hair texture, density, porosity and length.

Design Elements   *5*
Major components of an art form. In hair design, they are form, texture and color.

Design Principles   *21*
Arrangement patterns used in design. They include repetition, alternation, progression and contrast. In perm design, they may be applied to texture within zones, along the strand or throughout entire composition.

Disinfection   *68, 71, 72, 162, 164*
Infection control method that kills certain but not all microbes.

Distribute   *11, 14*
Direction the hair is combed or dispersed over the curve of the head; prepares the hair to be sectioned and then wrapped.

Disulfide Bond   *12, 29*
Important side bond containing sulfur; directly affected by perming and relaxing.

Double-Paper Technique   *54*
End paper wrapping technique that incorporates two end papers—one on the top and one on the bottom; also known as double-flat technique and is considered a protective technique for color-treated and fragile hair.

Draping   *69, 163*
Procedure used to protect client's skin and clothing and helps prevent skin irritation or burns.

Elasticity   *44, 143*
Ability of hair to stretch and return to its original shape without breaking.

End Paper   *54*
Porous paper used to control the hair ends and keep hair smoothly wrapped around the perm tool.

End Perming   *20*
Positions permed texture away from the base or at the ends of the hairstrand only.

Endothermic Perm   *7*
Acid perm used to speed up the processing time; heat is added to cause the pH to rise gradually; e.g., placing a plastic cap on the client and then under a pre-heated dryer.

Exothermic Perm   *33*
Self-timing and self-heating; uses an additive that creates heat through a chemical reaction mixed with perm solution; ranges from acidic to alkaline.

Glyceryl Monothioglycolate   *7*
Thioglycolic derivative; found in acid waves.

Half-Off Base   *52, 53*
Base control position in which the tool sits directly on its lower parting. The result is a lifted base. This most commonly used base control for perming avoids splitting between rods.

Ionic/Heat Perm   *33*
Perm that uses a computer to digitally control the temperature of each perm rod, giving the stylist a greater degree of control over the whole perming process; often referred to as a "digital perm."

Low-/No-Thio Perm   *33*
Perm that has cysteine hydrochloride as its reducing agent; available for people who may have an allergic reaction to thioglycolic acid, which is found in both alkaline and acid perms.

Neutralizer   *29, 34*
Product used in perming that fixes, locks in, restores and bonds to make new shape of hair permanent; acid-balanced neutralizing shampoo or stabilizer product used in a relaxer service to lock hair in a straighter shape.

Neutralizing   *57, 152*
Step in the perm or relaxer process that locks hair into its new shape while lowering the pH of the hair.

No-Lye Relaxer   *68*
Product that contains a derivative of sodium hydroxide or bisulfate; contains calcium, potassium, guanidine or lithium hydroxide as the active ingredient.

Normalizing Conditioner   *135*
Product used to close the cuticle after alkaline chemical services.

Off Base   *52, 53*
Tool or curl sits below the bottom parting of the base, creating minimum base strength and the least volume or lift.

On Base   *52, 53*
Tool or curl is centered between the top and bottom partings of the base; results in most volume and strongest base strength; full base.

One-Two Bricklay Pattern   *23*
Perm tools positioned in a staggered configuration; used to create consistent curl and help avoid splits between the bases.

Overlap (Croquignole) Wrapping Technique   *16, 49*
The process of rotating or revolving hair around a tool from the ends of the hairstrand up to the base.

Partial Perm   *24, 50*
Involves adding texture to areas such as the fringe, crown and nape; also called zonal perm.

Partial Relaxer   *125, 148*
Relaxer applied only to selected areas of the head; used mainly when the nape area and sides are closely tapered or when the perimeter hairline is frizzy; also called a zonal relaxer.

PIVOT POINT

EDUCATION DEVELOPMENT   **Janet Fisher // Sabine Held-Perez // Vasiliki A. Stavrakis**

Markel Artwell
Eileen Dubelbeis
Brian Fallon
Melissa Holmes
Lisa Luppino
Paul Suttles
Amy Gallagher
Lisa Kersting
Jamie Nabielec
Vic Piccolotto
Ericka Thelin
Jane Wegner

EDITORIAL   **Maureen Spurr // Wm. Bullion // Deidre Glover**

Liz Bagby
Jack Bernin
Lori Chapman

DESIGN & PRODUCTION   **Jennifer Eckstein // Rick Russell // Danya Shaikh**

Joanna Jakubowicz
Denise Podlin
Annette Baase
Agnieszka Hansen
Kristine Palmer
Tiffany Wu

PROJECT MANAGEMENT   **Jenny Allen // Ken Wegrzyn**

DIGITAL DEVELOPMENT

John Bernin
Javed Fouch
Anna Fehr
Matt McCarthy
Marcia Noriega
Corey Passage
Herb Potzus

Pivot Point also wishes to take this opportunity to acknowledge the many contributors and product concept testers who helped make this program possible.

INDUSTRY CONTRIBUTORS

Linda Burmeister
Esthetics

Jeanne Braa Foster
Dr. Dean Foster
Eyes on Cancer

Mandy Gross
Nails

Andrea D. Kelly, MA, MSW
University of Delaware

Rosanne Kinley
Infection Control
National Interstate Council

Lynn Maestro
Cirépil by Perron Rigot, Paris

Andrzej Matracki
World and European
Men's Champion

MODERN SALON

Rachel Molepske
Look Good Feel Better, PBA
CUT IT OUT, PBA

Peggy Moon
Liaison to Regulatory and Testing

Robert Richards
Fashion Illustrations

Clif St. Germain, Ph.D
Educational Consultant

Andis Company

International Dermal Institute

HairUWear Inc.

Lock & Loaded Men's Grooming

PRODUCT CONCEPT TESTING

Central Carolina
Community College
Millington, North Carolina

Gateway Community Colleges
Phoenix, Arizona

MC College
Edmonton, Alberta

Metro Beauty Academy
Allentown, Pennsylvania

Rowan Cabarrus
Community College
Kannapolis, North Carolina

Sunstate Academy of
Cosmetology and Massage
Ft. Myers, Florida

The Salon Professional Academy
Kokomo, Indiana

TONI&GUY Hairdressing Academy
Costa Mesa, California
Plano, Texas

Xenon Academy
Omaha, NE
Grand Island, NE

LEADERSHIP TEAM

Robert Passage
Chairman and CEO

Robert J. Sieh
Senior Vice President,
Finance and Operations

Judy Rambert
Vice President, Education

Kevin Cameron
Senior Vice President,
Education and Marketing

R.W. Miller
Vice President, Domestic Sales
and Field Education

Jan Laan
Vice President, International
Business Development

Katy O'Mahony
Director, Human Resources

In addition, we give special thanks to the North American Regulating agencies whose careful work protects us as well as our clients, enhancing the high quality of our work. These agencies include Occupational Health and Safety Agency (OSHA) and the U.S. Environmental Protection Agency (EPA). *Pivot Point Fundamentals* promotes use of their policies and procedures.

Pivot Point International would like to express our SPECIAL THANKS to the inspired visual artisans of Creative Commons, without whose talents this book of beauty would not be possible.